Behind the One-Way Mirror

Advances in the Practice of Strategic Therapy

Cloé Madanes

Behind the One-Way Mirror

Advances in the Practice of Strategic Therapy

Jossey-Bass Publishers

San Francisco   •   London   •   1986

BEHIND THE ONE-WAY MIRROR
Advances in the Practice of Strategic Therapy
by Cloé Madanes

Copyright © 1984 by: Jossey-Bass Inc., Publishers
433 California Street
San Francisco, California 94104
&
Jossey-Bass Limited
28 Banner Street
London EC1Y 8QE

Library of Congress Cataloging in Publication Data

Madanes, Cloé.
Behind the one-way mirror.

(The Jossey-Bass social and behavioral science series)
Bibliography: p. 189
Includes index.
1. Psychotherapy. 2. Psychotherapy—Case studies.
3. Family psychotherapy. 4. Family psychotherapy—Case
studies. I. Title. II. Series.
RC480.M28   1984   616.89′14   83-49266
ISBN 0-87589-599-9 (alk. paper)

Manufactured in the United States of America

The paper in this book meets the guidelines for
permanence and durability of the Committee on
Production Guidelines for Book Longevity of the
Council on Library Resources.

JACKET DESIGN BY WILLI BAUM

FIRST EDITION
First printing: March 1984
Second printing: September 1984
Third printing: April 1986

Code 8409

The Jossey-Bass
Social and Behavioral Science Series

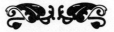

To my mother, Ida Salita de Madanes, with love and gratitude

Preface

This book is about an approach to therapy that developed from a concern with power and with the metaphors expressed by symptoms. These concerns are the point of departure for new ways of understanding the specificity of symptoms and new indirect strategies of therapy.

Chapter One develops the concept of metaphorical sequences of interaction, of the "planning ahead" involved in symptomatic behavior, and of the hierarchical incongruity that results when helplessness is a source of power. The chapter presents two case examples involving indirect, playful interventions.

Chapter Two explores the possibility that relations between two people are dependent on third party involvements. A conflictual interaction between a parent and a child, for example, may be a metaphor for and replace the conflictual interaction between the parent and another child. The author discusses the way tacit contracts for the distribution of benefits in an ongoing relationship are related to issues of hierarchy and power. Two indirect strategies are presented with case examples in which humor is used to change metaphors, redistribute benefits, and renegotiate contracts.

Chapter Three introduces an untapped resource in the mental health field: the child as therapist to the parents. The approach is indicated when parents present a problem, whether or not their children are also symptomatic. Children are put in charge of some aspect of the parents' lives and are given responsibility to effect change. They are given power to advise the parents, to offer the parents love and caring, to influence them to emulate the competent and caring behavior of their children, and to provoke the parents to change so that the children no longer need to be in charge. Three case examples are presented.

Chapter Four is a discussion of humor in therapy and is illustrated with numerous case examples. The therapist's ability to be optimistic and to see what is funny or appealing in a grim situation is what makes change possible. Communicating at multiple levels or being inconsistent and illogical may appear humorous and be therapeutic.

Chapter Five presents eight dimensions for conceptualizing a problem brought to therapy and describes ten paradoxical strategies, with case examples illustrating each strategy. The emphasis is on how to choose the strategy that is best suited for each problem based on how the problem is conceptualized.

This volume includes thirty case examples covering a wide age range and a great variety of problems. In these cases, I was the supervisor, observing each session from behind a one-way mirror, planning the approach, calling the therapists on the phone during the sessions or asking them to come out of the sessions for discussions, and in these ways guiding the therapists through the therapy. Similarly, in this book the reader is guided through the case studies in order to understand step by step what I was thinking behind the one-way mirror during each interview, what hypotheses were formulated and which were discarded, and how a strategy was planned and carried out.

Acknowledgments

The training program in which I taught took place at the Family Therapy Institute of Washington, D.C. The therapists in

the cases presented in the book were professionals in the field—
psychologists, social workers, psychiatrists, and psychiatric
nurses—who were senior therapists at the institute or trainees
learning this particular approach. The senior therapists were:
Richard Belson, Judith Mazza, Marcha Ortiz, and Neil Schiff.
The trainees were: Galen Alessi, Judy Birch, Linda Carter, Marvin Chelst, Patricia Davidge, Patrick Fleming, Rochelle Herman,
Heidi Hsia, Gerald Hunt, Rao Inaganti, Vicki Karlin, June Kaufman, Bette Marcus, Chip Olhaver, Joe Pastore, Penny Purcell,
Frank Schindler, Lyn Stycinski, Carol Waser, and Richard
Whiteside. I am indebted to them and to all my other students
for contributing to the development of the ideas expressed in
this book.

Bethesda, Maryland   Cloé Madanes
January 1984

Contents

The Author

Cloé Madanes is co-director of the Family Therapy Institute of Washington, D.C. She received the degree of "Licienciada" in psychology from the University of Buenos Aires in 1965. Madanes has been a teacher and supervisor of therapy for more than twelve years. She is the author of *Strategic Family Therapy* (Jossey-Bass, 1981) and of numerous papers, among them: "Protection, Paradox and Pretending"; "Family Ties of Heroin Addicts"; and "Marital Therapy When a Symptom Is Presented by a Spouse." Madanes has also produced several films and gives workshops on her approach to therapy both in the United States and abroad.

Behind the One-Way Mirror

Advances in the Practice of Strategic Therapy

1

Understanding
and Changing
Relationships

When a child says "My head hurts," he may be referring to
more than one kind of pain. He* may be saying that his feelings are hurt or that his mother is suffering, or he may be
asking for help with his homework. A symptom is a message
and, as such, it may have a second referent different from the
one explicitly stated. The second referent, the second meaning, may refer to someone other than the person expressing
the message.

Metaphor in Families

Just as a message may have a second referent, so may a
sequence of interaction. That is, a sequence of interaction between two people may be a metaphor for and take the place
of a different sequence of interaction between two other people (Madanes, 1981b). As an example, a father comes home
from work upset, worried, and anxious about his work because

*The author uses *he* for reasons of convenience and acknowl-
edges the inequity of the traditional use of the masculine pronoun.

he is about to be fired. As his wife reassures him and comforts him, their son develops an asthma attack. The father then begins to comfort and reassure the son in the same way that the wife had been comforting and reassuring him. The interaction between father and son replaces and is a metaphor for the interaction between wife and husband. At the time that the father is reassuring the child, the wife cannot be reassuring the husband. One sequence has replaced the other.

The concept of metaphorical sequences leads logically to the idea that the variations in the focus of interaction in a family follow cycles. Sometimes, for example, a sequence will focus on the father's work difficulties, sometimes on the symptom of the child, sometimes on problems with an in-law or on money difficulties. But the sequence of interaction will remain the same. For instance, there might always be someone helpless involved, who exhibits involuntary behavior, and someone helpful, who fails to help. This sequence might appear in various ways in a family and involve various dyads, with each sequence representing metaphorically another sequence. This is quite different from thinking about the metaphor in a dream or in a symbol. A different order of concepts is involved when we talk about the metaphoric aspects of sequences of behavior.

This progression in thinking about metaphors is relevant in various ways to the way a family is approached in therapy. In a first interview, it is useful to discover the metaphor expressed by the presenting problem and by the interaction around the presenting problem. This is not just of theoretical or intellectual interest in understanding a family; it is a practical issue, because the strategy developed to solve the problem will be based on this understanding. When a family presents a problem, it is useful to think: If the problem is a metaphor for another behavior, for what does it stand? Who else in the family has a similar problem? What interaction is not possible because this interaction is taking place? To what interaction does this situation lead? What is the situation that is replacing another situation? To answer these questions, one must understand metaphors.

Planning Ahead

These ideas about metaphor in families led to a second concept: the idea of planning ahead (Madanes, 1981b). Even though this is a simple idea, it has only developed recently as a result of a change in focus from past causes of current behavior to anticipated consequences of that behavior. The sequence is this: a father comes home from work upset and worried that he might be fired. His wife tries to help him and reassure him. Their child develops a symptom, and the father pulls himself together and behaves like a competent parent, giving his child medication, comfort, and caring. At that point, he is no longer a man afraid of losing his job. He has become a concerned father and a mature adult in relation to his child.

Is it possible that the child has planned this behavior to help his father pull himself together? Could the child have developed a symptom to free the mother from having to try to help the father? Is it possible that the child could plan ahead in this way? The question is not merely theoretical. If a therapist can develop such an hypothesis when interviewing a family, he can begin to understand the child's plan. To understand this plan, it is best to focus on the helpfulness and protectiveness of the child. In what way is the child's plan helpful, and what is unfortunate about this mode of helpfulness? The child's plan to help the parents often creates a worse problem than the one the child is intending to solve. The unfortunate nature of this helpfulness is what must be changed. This helpfulness causes the power of the child over the parents to be exaggerated. The child exerts power and influence inappropriate to his situation as a child in the family. Through problem behavior, the child can change a parent from a helpless, upset person into a competent, helpful parent.

When the child's plan is known, the strategy for solving the problem becomes immediately apparent: to arrange for a new sequence of interaction by which the same end can be achieved without the symptom. Then the child need no longer exhibit the symptom. It is difficult to think that a child has the

intelligence to plan such a sequence. Yet, it is difficult to think
that a child does *not* have that intelligence. Children are intelligent in ways that are more complex than that. It is rather simple, for example, for a child to anticipate how his father will
respond to his behavior; curiously, however, it has taken quite a
long time to develop the idea that children do plan ahead in
these ways. The issue arises: If the child plans, is such planning
done consciously? Is it deliberate? At times it is. Children have
been known to explain how and why they plan symptomatic
behavior. For example: "If I am sick, then my father will not
drink that day," or "he will not go away," or "my mother
will not go out with her girlfriend." But the question arises as
to whether the child really plans or whether it is the father who
elicits this kind of behavior from the child so that he can pull
himself together and think of himself as a caring father rather
than as a failing adult. Or does the mother elicit the behavior in
the child so she can be free from having to support her husband
in his difficulties? What is the truth is really not the question.
The important consideration is what kind of punctuation of the
events will best lead to designing a strategy for change. Some
therapists prefer to think of the child as the initiator of sequences and some prefer to think of the parents. Probably all
are involved, although this is not necessarily the case. The issue
is what kind of thinking will help the therapist develop a strategy to solve the problem. It is important to remember that a
therapist is only seeking a workable hypothesis, one that will
help him to develop a plan to interfere with the unfortunate
plan of the family or the child.

The task of identifying helpfulness is complex. A child,
for example, behaves in symptomatic ways that are helpful to
his parents. The parents focus on the child to help him overcome his problems. This helpfulness on the part of the parents
perpetuates the function of the child's symptomatic behavior,
and he becomes more helpless in a way that is helpful to the
parents. The ways in which the child protects the parents make
the child appear helpless because of his disturbed behavior, yet
he is powerful as a helper to the family.

Hierarchy

A third concept regarding metaphorical sequences has to do with hierarchy. When problem behavior is metaphorical of other problem behavior, or when a sequence of interaction is metaphorical of another sequence, or when a child plans to be helpful to the parents in indirect ways, there is an incongruity in the hierarchical organization of the family. That is, when the child carries out a plan to help the parents in indirect ways with issues that are important to them, the child takes a position of leadership in the family; this is incongruous with the fact that the parents support the child, care for him, provide him with guidance, and so on. There is a dual hierarchy in the family: In one, the child is in charge; in the other, the parents are in charge of the child. The task of the therapist is to correct this hierarchy and reorganize the family so that the parents are in a superior position and help and support the child and the child does not take care of the parents in unfortunate ways. It is not sufficient for the therapist to come into the situation and correct the hierarchy in relation to himself, no matter how much authority he has over the child. The problem is in relation to the parents, not to the therapist, and the parents must correct the hierarchy. The therapist must create a situation in which this can take place.

Therapists have developed various ways of dealing with this dilemma, such as encouraging parents to ignore the problem behavior or having them pay attention to the child and reward him only when he does not exhibit the symptom. Behavior therapists have helped parents develop a set of contingencies that encourage and reward appropriate, nonsymptomatic behavior.

Reframing the problem and challenging both parents and child is one approach used by Minuchin in his work with the families of psychosomatic patients, particularly anorectics. "The therapist mobilizes the parents to treat their daughter as a rebellious adolescent, not as an incompetent, ineffective invalid" (Minuchin, Rosman, and Baker, 1978, p. 96). The anorectic's symptoms are reframed as acts of power and manipulation. This approach supports the hierarchical organization of the family through therapeutic operations that "challenge" enmeshment and overprotection and support individuation and clear boundaries between the parental and child subsystems. The therapist also challenges conflict avoidance by these families, preventing cross-generational coalitions and supporting "the parents' right to establish rules in the house and the child's right to command respect for age-appropriate autonomy" (Minuchin, Rosman, and Baker, 1978, p. 105). In this approach, use of the child as a means to detour conflicts between the parents is challenged, and triangulation sequences in which the child repeatedly finds himself in situations in which he must choose between the parents are blocked.

Paradoxical techniques have been used to deal with the dilemma of the power struggle between parents and child. In these techniques, the parents are asked to request that the child actually try to have the symptom on purpose, so that the child, instead of involuntarily having the symptom and being supported and reassured by his parents, tries to voluntarily have the symptom at the request of the parents (Madanes, 1981b). The idea is that the more the child tries to have the symptom, the less likely he is to have it. The interaction between parents and child changes from a situation in which the child involuntarily has a symptom while the parents ineffectually attempt to prevent it to one in which the parents encourage the child to have the symptom and the child is unable to have it. Selvini Palazzoli, Cecchin, Prata, and Boscolo (1978) use a paradoxical approach in which the therapist defines the symptomatic behavior and the parents' helpfulness as positive and then requests that all family members continue to behave in their usual way, suggesting that this will best maintain the union of the family group.

A different approach to the problem of the child's symptom and of the power derived from the symptom is based on an integration of ideas about metaphor, planning ahead, and hierarchy. The approach is part of a strategic therapy focused on designing an intervention that will shift the family organization so that the presenting problem is no longer necessary. This is a problem-solving approach in which a specific strategy is designed for each presenting problem. The two strategies presented here illustrate how to identify and understand both the metaphorical sequences of interaction and the helpful planning ahead involved in symptomatic behavior of children. In this approach, the therapist designs an intervention to raise the parents in the hierarchy so that they are helping and protecting the child and the child is not helping the parents in inappropriate ways. It is possible to use direct interventions in which the parents are overtly supported in a superior position. However, the examples presented here involve indirect interventions in which metaphors are used and the relationship between parents and child is redefined in playful ways.*

Pretending to be Nurses

It is not uncommon for parent and child to present the same symptomatic behavior. Correcting the hierarchy in such cases is particularly difficult, since the symptom equalizes the positions of parent and child. One approach to the therapy is to create an imaginary reality in which hierarchical differences are clear.

A pediatrician referred a mother and daughter to family therapy.** The daughter was ten years old and had been in and out of the hospital during the five years since she had been diagnosed as having juvenile diabetes. She had been hospitalized repeatedly for extreme weakness or diabetic coma. The pediatrician thought that if the child were properly cared for—her urine tested twice a day and her insulin shots given—the diabetes would be kept under control and the child could lead a normal life; she thought that the mother neglected the child even though the mother insisted that she did not and that she always

***

*The therapists in these cases were Rao Inaganti, M.D., and Linda Carter, Ph.D. The therapies were conducted at the Department of Psychiatry, University of Maryland Hospital, and the Family Therapy Institute of Washington, D.C.

**This case was described elsewhere (Madanes, 1981a) from a somewhat different perspective.

followed the doctor's instructions. The problem was further complicated by the fact that the mother was also diabetic and apparently had neglected to take care of herself—to the point that she had lost all her teeth, was losing her eyesight, and had a heart condition.

The Visiting Nurses Association had been unsuccessfully involved with the family in numerous contacts. The pediatrician had referred the case to a behavior modification program in a department of pediatrics, but the psychologist there had concluded that the child was not amenable to psychotherapy because she was too manipulative and used her diabetes to attract attention. The pediatrician, however, persisted in her attempts to help the child and referred the case to family therapy with the hope that the mother could be moved to take care of her child. The father had divorced the mother and had no contact with the child. The mother was on public assistance.

Even before the first interview, the supervisor was able to make certain assumptions about the case. It was clear that there was a great deal of antagonism between the mother and not only the pediatrician but probably all the physicians and nurses with whom she had come in contact during the previous five years. Probably the doctors and nurses had repeatedly, explicitly or implicitly, accused the mother of not following their instructions and had insisted that she do so, while the mother had repeatedly denied disobeying them and promised to follow their orders. However, she failed to do so. The issue presented to therapy was one that is always present in cases of neglect and abuse: how to raise parents in the hierarchy so that they will behave as competent, caring parents in relation to the child without putting them down by pointing out their shortcomings and telling them what to do. Attempts to tell a parent how to be responsible often only worsen the situation by putting the parent down even more. The issue was how the therapist would put the mother benevolently in charge of her daughter without exercising authority over her in a way that would prevent her from taking charge. The problem was how to put the mother in charge of the daughter when her reaction to being put in charge was to rebel against the authorities who were putting her in that position—as is often the situation in cases of neglect. It was clear that, if the family therapy were to succeed, there should be no implication that the mother had been neglectful in the past and no accusations, and the mother would have to be moved indirectly toward competent parental behavior.

Apparently, over a period of five years, many competent, intelligent professionals had attempted to help this mother and daughter; it was reasonable to assume that every possible direct method of influence had been used. These methods probably included explanations of: the nature of the illness; the rules for good medical care; the part played by diet, rest, urine testing, and insulin shots; the need for maintaining daily charts and for regular medical checkups; and the use of positive reinforcement to motivate the child to cooperate with the regime. All this had been to no avail. There was no reason to assume that the therapy would succeed using direct methods of influence where so many intelligent people had been unsuccessful. Indirect methods, however, might succeed in influencing mother and daughter where direct attempts had previously failed. The supervisor instructed the therapist before the first session not to argue with the mother or antagonize her in any way, since it was thought that others who had done so had failed to influence her.

As the supervisor thought about the problem before the beginning of the therapy, the question arose: Is it possible that the child goes into diabetic coma and gets herself into the hospital to help her mother? What could be helpful to the mother about the child's hospitalizations? A ten-year-old girl can take care of her urine testing perfectly well and can even give herself shots if she is of normal intelligence, as this girl was, according to the psychological reports. Could it be that this girl was not taking care of herself in an attempt to help her mother? Ths supervisor noted that the referral came from a general hospital, not a children's hospital. It was possible that when the child was in the hospital and the mother visited her, or when the mother frequently had to take the child to the hospital, she would be inclined to take the opportunity to see her own physician in another department of the same hospital. This seemed a possibility, and the supervisor decided to pursue this line of thinking. Perhaps the child did not take care of herself and was so frequently hospitalized because in that way she could put her mother in contact with doctors who might help her take better care of herself. That is, it was assumed that the mother avoided going to the doctor for her own health; however, if she had to take the child to the hospital or visit her there, she probably consulted about herself also. In this way, the child planned ahead to help her mother through symptomatic behavior that was a source of power over the mother and a metaphor for the mother's own helplessness and neglect of herself. However, this helpfulness by the child was self-destructive and dangerous. The problem was how to arrange for the daughter to protect the mother and get her to take care of herself without harming her own body to do so. The child's need to be helpful could not be avoided due to the chronic nature of the mother's illness, but a more direct, less costly helpfulness could be arranged.

The goal of the therapy was to solve the problem of the mother's neglect of her daughter. In terms of metaphor, the child's helplessness and incompetence in taking care of herself were thought to be a metaphor for the mother's helplessness and incompetence in caring for the child and for herself. In terms of planning ahead, the girl was thought to plan for the mother's medical care by putting her in contact with physicians through her own frequent illnesses and hospitalizations. In terms of hierarchy, the child exercised a tyranny over the mother through the helplessness of her precarious health, the emergency hospitalizations, and the humiliation suffered by the mother for being considered neglectful.

The therapy would take place in stages. First, the therapist would help move the mother toward behaving competently and helpfully toward the daughter so that in a later stage the child would behave in ways that would be metaphorical of the mother's competence and not of her helplessness. As the mother cared properly for the girl, her position in the family hierarchy would be raised. In the second stage, the therapist would arrange for the daughter to help the mother in appropriate direct ways, without harming herself. In the third stage, a method would be established by which mother and daughter could alternately take care of each other, each without neglecting herself or the other person, and without the need to continue in therapy. This would be the general strategy of the therapy; the specific techniques that would be used to carry it out were not known. The plan was that the therapist would begin the first interview by talking with mother and daughter about the girl's diabetes and, while observing, the supervisor would devise specific techniques for carrying out the plan. It was necessary to wait for the family to provide a metaphor on which to base an indirect, playful strategy.

Mother and daughter came to the first interview. The daughter was a delicate, beautiful, angel-like, frail blonde. The mother was overweight, toothless, and wrinkled, and she looked at her daughter in awe, as if wondering how she could have produced such a lovely child. The therapist explained that the pediatrician had referred them because she was concerned that the child's diabetes was not under control, even though the child could be expected to lead a totally normal life if her urine were tested regularly and insulin shots were given. The mother said that she knew this and that the girl was certainly testing her own urine and taking the shots every day, although that morning she had not done so. The mother's tone and attitude were slightly belligerent, as if she were ready to argue with anyone who questioned the veracity of her statements.

The mother's account clearly was not exactly the truth, as otherwise there would have been no hospitalizations and no reason for the pediatrician's concern. The therapist, however, was prepared not to question the veracity of the mother's statement so that he could establish a cooperative rather than an antagonistic relationship with her.

As the therapist talked with the mother and daughter, the supervisor behind the one-way mirror observed the love with which the mother looked at the child. The mother was dressed as if her clothes had been donated by charity, while the daughter was expensively dressed. The supervisor thought of how this child was all that the mother had in life and of how afraid she

must be of losing the child's love. It was clear that this was not
a mother who was neglectful because she did not love her
daughter. On the contrary, it could be hypothesized that she
loved her daughter so much that she was incapable of enforc-
ing the basic rules that were necessary to control the diabetes.
If the girl did not feel like taking an insulin shot, the mother
probably did not force her to take it; if she did not want to give
a urine sample, the urine probably went untested. In this way
the mother did not risk the possibility of causing the child dis-
comfort and pain and losing her love. As the supervisor was
thinking about this, the mother said, with a touch of jealousy in
her voice, that the child was more cooperative with the visiting
nurse, for whom she would always produce a urine sample, than
she was with the mother. This statement by the mother provided the metaphor that was the basis for the techniques that
were developed to solve the problem.

The supervisor instructed the therapist to say that the girl
had proven to be irresponsible in the past in testing her own
urine, and, consequently, now the mother had to be in charge
of testing the child's urine and giving her the shots. In fact, the
mother should imagine that she was a nurse. The mother laughed
at this, pleased, and said "Oh, yeah, you could see that, could
you?" not without certain pride. This was a good sign: If the
therapist managed to change the situation into one of make-
believe, giving the mother an imaginary higher status as a nurse,
the mother would respond by living up to the situation and behaving more competently. To this mother, who did not have a
high school education, being a nurse was as high a status as she
could possibly imagine.

The therapist then said, "You have to take care of this
patient," pointing to the daughter, and proceeded to make a
chart that the mother would keep of the daughter's progress.
She would regularly show this chart to the therapist, who would
be the doctor checking that the nurse did her job properly. The
therapist continued, saying that from now on the mother would
be not Mrs. Robins but Nurse Robins and the girl would be not
the daughter but the patient. The girl would no longer be responsible for her own urine tests and shots. The mother would

be in charge. The therapist said, "Think of yourself as a nurse, not as a mother. A nurse sternly tells the patient, 'You have to do this,' and the patient does it, because the doctor told her so. Imagine that you are a nurse and fill out this chart like a nurse does." The mother agreed. From then on, the therapist, who was really a doctor, referred to himself as "the doctor," in the third person, the mother as "the nurse," and the daughter as "the patient." The chart was prepared to show the schedule by which the urine had been tested, the results of the testing, and the schedule and dosage in which the insulin shots were given.

The therapist added that, in fact, the mother was like a nurse in that she knew so much about diabetes because she had the same problem. Actually, what the mother needed was a nurse's uniform, and the therapist could provide that. The mother laughed and said that he would never find one big enough for her, but the therapist assured her that he would and excused himself from the room. He came back with the nurse's uniform and gave it to the mother, who was very pleased and immediately put it on, with the help of the little girl. The therapist said that every morning the mother should put on the uniform and become Nurse Robins. Whenever she was wearing the uniform she would no longer be a mother—she would be a nurse. She then would wake up the child and take her to the bathroom to check her urine. The therapist asked the mother to show him in a pretend way in the session how she would do this. The mother took the daughter's hand and walked across the room to a pretend bathroom and pretended to test the urine. When mother and daughter returned to their seats, the therapist asked the mother to note the results of the test on the chart so she could show the record to the doctor. Then he asked the mother to pretend that it was evening and to give the child the insulin. Mother and daughter did this with quite extraordinary realism. They again returned to their seats and the mother was asked to note the amount of insulin on the chart. Then the therapist asked the mother to hug and kiss the daughter because she had been a good girl. (It was important to do this because, when a hierarchy is incorrect in terms of authority and caring, it is also incorrect in terms of affect.) After this, mother and daughter pretended that it was nighttime, and the urine was tested again. The mother then spontaneously kissed the daughter and wrote the results of the test on the chart.

Through all this pretending, mother and daughter were pleased and cheerful. The mother was very cooperative and not at all antagonistic, as she had been at the beginning of the interview. As a nurse, she was very compliant with the doctor's instructions. The therapist instructed the mother to bring the chart (which he had placed in a folder so that it looked like a doctor's record) to every interview so he could check it.

That was the end of the first session. Therapist and supervisor thought that with this intervention, the hierarchy had been corrected and the mother's status raised sufficiently so that she would competently take care of her daughter. However, something also needed to be done about the mother's neglect of her own illness and the child's need to help her mother. This intervention took place in the second interview.

Mother and daughter arrived at the second session a week later looking very nice, with their hair curled. The mother spontaneously showed the chart to the therapist and was pleased because the child's diabetes was under control. She had also brought the bottle of sticks to show the therapist what she used to test the urine. The therapist congratulated the mother, saying that she was a good nurse, and asked her to show him how she did her nursing at home. The mother put on the nurse's uniform, which she had brought, and the girl helped her tie it. Mother and daughter pretended in the same way they had in the first interview, but with even greater detail and drama. The therapist was appreciative and asked the mother to continue doing the same and to keep the charts not only to show him but also to show the pediatrician.

The first stage of the therapy had been successfully completed, in that the mother had moved from a helpless position to one of responsibility. It was now possible to arrange for the daughter to behave in ways metaphorical of the mother's competence rather than of her helplessness. The daughter could also now begin to help the mother in appropriate and not unfortunate ways. This was the second stage of the therapy.

The therapist asked the mother to take off the uniform because he wanted to talk with the mother, not with the nurse. He then asked her how frequently she went to the doctor for herself and whether she tested her own urine and took the insulin shots. The mother said that she had to go to the hospital every three months for herself, although she had to go more frequently for her daughter. She said that she did take the insulin shots regularly but did not test her urine because the sticks were too expensive and she could not afford them. The therapist explained how she could cut the sticks in half longitudinally so that both mother and daughter could use one stick. The therapist also promised that he would try to provide them with free sticks or with a less expensive method.

The girl was very interested in this conversation and volunteered information, explaining that the mother should be testing her urine. The therapist said that the child seemed very concerned and mother and daughter agreed, saying that the girl had even "told on" the mother to the doctor and the nurse at the hospital. This confirmed the hypothesis about the child's concern for and protectiveness of the mother.

The therapist then gave the child a little nurse's uniform and asked her to put it on so she could play a game in which she was a nurse to her mother. He asked the daughter to pretend to take the mother to the bathroom for the urine testing, just as the mother had pretended to take her. They did this, and then the child pretended to remind the mother and supervise her while she took the insulin shots. The daughter was asked to hug and kiss the mother because she had behaved properly. She then pretended it was nighttime and tested the mother's urine again. Throughout the procedure, the girl was delighted, and the mother attempted to instruct the daughter on how she, the child, was to take care of the mother. In this way, the mother made it clear that this was "pretend" and the daughter was not "really" in charge. This is a usual response to a reversal of the family hierarchy by a therapist. The parent reacts by taking charge and correcting the hierarchy. In this case, the mother's reaction was interesting in that it was similar to the paradox "I want you to dominate me," since the mother was instructing the child on how the child should supervise the mother. The therapist ignored the mother's attempts to take charge and remained in the role of the doctor instructing the little nurse on how to take care of her patient.

The therapist prepared a folder that the daughter, as nurse, would keep on the mother's progress. The girl quickly understood how to keep the chart and was very pleased with what she was to do. The daughter could now be a metaphor for her mother by behaving as a caring nurse rather than as a helpless diabetic. The therapist asked both nurses to shake hands and to tell each other that they would do their jobs. The mother shook hands with the daughter and said: "Mommy will do our job." Although this was exactly what the therapist was after, he pretended not to hear and asked them to shake hands again while each said: "I promise that I will do my job." They promised to do so and shook hands.

In the next two sessions, mother and daughter reported that they had followed all the instructions, and they brought in their charts showing that their diabetes was under control. The therapist congratulated them and asked for a performance, and they were pleased to oblige. The girl, who had had some difficulties at school, was now doing much better and getting good grades, and the mother was participating in school activities. She had volunteered to help on the playground and in organizing a school picnic, was involved with other mothers, and was coming out of her isolation. The mother explained that they had gone to the hospital and shown the charts to the doctors and nurses, who were very pleased.

At this point, the end of the academic year was approaching, the training of the therapist was coming to an end and he was moving to a different job, and the supervisor was going away on vacation. The supervisor pondered what to do with this family. Even though they were doing well, ending the therapy appeared premature, given the long history of disturbance. To transfer to another therapist might mean that all that had been accomplished could be ruined. At this time also, from the medical point of view, a transfer to a new physician with whom the mother could have a fresh start could be beneficial. The therapist discovered that there was a small clinic, mainly run by nurses, in the mother's neighborhood, to which the medical supervision of the child's diabetes could be transferred. He asked the mother whether she would be interested in transferring, and the mother said that it would be more convenient. It was thought then that it might be possible to arrange to transfer not just the medical but also the therapeutic aspect of the case to a nurse in this new clinic. The new nurse could be like the head nurse, with the mother and daughter under her, and she could visit them at home and make sure that they were taking care of each other.

With this plan in mind, a last appointment was set up, to which a nurse from the clinic was invited. The nurse was told only that she should come to the University of Maryland Hospital to arrange for the transfer of a case of juvenile diabetes. The problem was how to explain the procedure of pretending to be nurses to her so that she would be willing to assume responsibility for continuing with this strategy. In explaining the history of the case and the therapy plan, the therapist had to be careful not to make the nurse feel that she was not qualified to take over such a difficult case with a psychotherapy component that she was not trained to handle; perhaps if the nurse were introduced directly to the mother and the daughter, without being given any previous information or preparation, and witnessed their performances as nurses to each other, she would be emotionally moved and willing to take responsibility and play the part of the head nurse. The interview was conducted on that basis.

Mother and daughter had brought their charts and showed how both their conditions were under control. The therapist explained the charts to the nurse who would supervise them from then on. He asked mother and daughter to do both of their pretend dramatizations for the nurse to see, since she also would check regularly to see that each was nurse to the other. Mother and daughter put on a nice performance for the nurse. The daughter then said that she had an opportunity to go to camp for a few weeks but was reluctant to go because she was concerned that she would not be nurse to her mother during that time. The therapist asked the nurse to promise the child that she would check on the mother three times a week while the daughter was gone and keep the chart for her. The nurse promised, and the child was reassured.

The therapist said that he would check regularly with the nurse to see that mother and daughter were all right and that he also would keep in touch with the family.

To summarize, at the beginning of therapy, the child's weakness and diabetic coma were expressing her unhappiness and her mother's unhappiness. They were a report on her internal feelings, as well as a command to the mother to take care of herself. The daughter neglected herself and became ill in a way that was metaphorical of the way the mother did not take care of her own illness or of the daughter. The pediatrician's complaints to the mother about her neglect of her child were metaphoric of the child's complaints to doctors and nurses about the mother's neglect of herself. The child's plan was to arrange, by being ill and hospitalized, that the mother would be in contact with doctors who might help her with her own illness. The daughter was helpless because of her illness, yet she was powerful as a helper to her mother. This helpfulness, however, was costly to herself and created a worse problem than the one it was intended to solve.

The strategy developed to solve the problem consisted of eliciting competent, caring behavior from the mother by giving her status and power in a make-believe way, which led to the mother taking charge of the child's diabetes in a real way. The mother was moved from a helpless position to one of responsibility. The child's need to help her mother was accepted, and she was provided with a playful but appropriate way to help the mother. When pretending to be a nurse, the child was behaving in ways that were metaphorical of the mother's competence and not of her helplessness.

In terms of the three concepts presented earlier in this chapter, at the beginning of the therapy the daughter was behaving in helpless and incompetent ways that were a metaphor for the mother's helplessness and incompetence. At the end of the therapy, the daughter was behaving in helpful and competent ways that were metaphorical of the mother's helpfulness and competence. At the beginning of the therapy, the daughter had a plan to help the mother by damaging her own body so that the mother might come into contact with physicians who could help her. By the end of the therapy, the daughter had an appropriate, successful plan to help her mother by pretending to be her nurse. In terms of hierarchy, at the beginning of the therapy the daughter was unpredictably in charge of the mother through crises and emergency visits to the hospital. By the end of the therapy, the daughter was in control of the mother only in a limited and predictable situation—when she wore the nurse's uniform.

From the point of view of the mother, at the beginning of the therapy she was behaving in a helpless and incompetent way. By the end of the therapy, she was helpful and competent, and she allowed the girl to be helpful to her. As she gained confidence in herself as a nurse to her daughter, she began to be caring and responsible in other areas of the girl's life.

For two years, mother and daughter were well and there were no hospitalizations. In the third year, the mother was hospitalized for heart failure, and shortly after that the daughter was also hospitalized in relation to her diabetes. By chance, the supervisor learned that a pediatrician was pressing charges against the mother for neglect and had arranged to give the child into foster care to a nurse who was caring for her in the hospital. The supervisor telephoned the pediatrician and asked her to withdraw the charges and to give her the opportunity to work once more with the family. Even though supervisor and pediatrician both worked out of the same university hospital, and even though it was explained that separating the child from the mother would only make it more difficult to control the diabetes, since the stress and sorrow would be unbearable to both, the pediatrician refused to withdraw the charges. The supervisor contacted mother and daughter and promised to help them. The ladies of the church to which the mother belonged hired a lawyer to defend her. On the day of the court hearing, an agreement was reached out of court, after much struggle. The supervisor would be given the opportunity to work with the family for four months while the child lived with her mother. Then there would be another hearing to determine whether or not she would be placed in foster care. The medical care would be provided by the same pediatrician who was pressing charges against the mother. It was impossible to reach a better agreement with the representative of the Department of Social Services, even though it was explained that, were the child to be placed in foster care, she would probably go into diabetic crisis to prove that the foster mother was not better than her own mother, and even though it was emphasized that a diabetic should not be stressed with threats of separation.

The problem for therapy now was how to protect mother and daughter from the attempts of professional helpers (pediatrician, nurses, and social workers) to violate their human rights and their rights as a family. The supervisor proposed to mother and daughter that the problem for therapy was now the child's fear of doctors due to her bad experience with the pediatrician who was trying to take her away from her mother. They agreed that this was the problem and cheerfully accepted the suggestion that they should be transferred to a more kindly pediatrician, who would provide a corrective experience in contrast to the previous trauma. The author contacted the Department of Social Services and explained that the child's emotional problem was now a fear of doctors and that this fear was extremely dangerous in the case of a chronic diabetic who would always need to be under doctors' care. The author also pointed out that it is a child's and mother's right to choose a pediatrician that they like. The social worker agreed and said that, as long as the new pediatrician was reputable, Social Services would accept the change, since families do have the right to choose their physician. A transfer was arranged to a more benevolent pediatrician, who gave strict control and supervision of the child to the mother. As this book goes to press, mother and daughter are well and trustful of the new doctor. The Department of Social Services has agreed to close the case if the new pediatrician reports in three months that the child is well taken care of. Only then will mother and daughter be relieved from the threat of separation and loss to which they were so unfairly subjected.

The Suicidal Sisters

Sometimes a child's problem behavior expresses meta-phorically the problem of a parent and helps the parents by shifting the family's focus of concern from a parent to the child. In this situation, the parents covertly ask for the child's help and the child covertly helps the parents through sympto-matic behavior.

When a child protects the parents through symptomatic behavior, he is helping them in a covert way. An approach to therapy is to encourage the parents to *pretend* to need the child's help and protection, rather than to actually need it. The child then can be encouraged to pretend to help the parents when the parents are pretending to need his help. The child will no longer need to behave in symptomatic ways in order to pro-tect the parents, since the parents' need for help will be a pre-tense and so will the child's helpfulness. In a pretend frame-work, parents and child will be involved with each other in a playful way.

A mother consulted because her fifteen-year-old daugh-ter, Amy, wanted to do "bodily harm to people" and her six-teen-year-old daughter, Beth, could not sleep at night. In the first interview, the therapist discovered that Amy had been scratching her wrists for some time, making superficial cuts with knives, bobby pins, paper clips, staples, and so on. Beth had previously written suicide notes. There were five daughters in the family between the ages of twelve and nineteen and one nine-year-old son. The father was a working man who was also going to college. The mother told the therapist on the phone that the father was too busy for and would be unwilling to come to therapy, but when the therapist called him he said he certainly would come and subsequently always came to the sessions. The mother worked a night shift as a nurse to pay debts that she had incurred for the family. She was always ex-hausted, because she also did all the housework with no help from the children. The mother was very young and attractive, as were the daughters, and they looked and behaved like sisters.

A supervisor other than the author was involved with the

case during the first five months of therapy. Several direct interventions were used during this time. The first was to organize a
twenty-four-hour suicide watch for Amy that involved all family members, who took turns watching her constantly. The
strategy was to dramatize the seriousness of the problem, since
the family seemed to minimize the seriousness of the suicide attempts. In one or two weeks the problem with Amy appeared
to be solved.

The focus of the therapy then shifted to schedules and
household responsibilities, since the mother was obviously
overburdened. The father was seen as uninvolved, angry, and excluded from a collusion among the women in the family. The
girls did nothing around the house, and the mother preferred
exhaustion to going after the girls to do some chores. The father
was put in charge of organizing the children with charts of
chores they were to do. This went well for a few weeks, and
then they slipped back to the previous disorganization.

An appointment was made to see the parents alone to resolve whatever issues were preventing them from organizing the
household. However, this meeting had to be postponed because
Beth said she needed help because she was an alcoholic, although she had recently stopped drinking, and she was having
problems in school. When this problem subsided, Amy said she
was moving out with her boyfriend. Then Beth had temper tantrums. The two girls took turns bringing up a problem every
time the therapist wanted to approach the parents' marriage.

The mother talked about how tired she was of everything
and how she felt like taking off and leaving the family. Apparently, she resented an affair that the husband had had at the beginning of the marriage. The mother was going out to bars with
an unmarried sister, and she was having thoughts about affairs.
When she talked about leaving the family, the father responded
impersonally, saying that she was too responsible to leave. The
mother said that she no longer had any feelings for him and was
thinking of leaving him in April. Several attempts to improve
the marriage were made, but to no avail. Every directive given
by the therapist was followed by the couple in a way that dis-
qualified the therapist. For example, when asked to go out to

dinner together, they went to McDonald's. When the father was asked to give the mother a gift, he gave her a cranberry dish.

In the fifth month of therapy, the family said that things had improved and they no longer felt the need to come to the sessions. Shortly afterward, the mother called the therapist and said that she had had a physical examination and was very frightened because there were signs of cancer. This turned out to be a false alarm, but a few days later she brought Amy to a session because once more she had cut her arms with a knife. The mother was vague about this episode, as she had been about most others, and it was an older sister, Meg, who had taken care of Amy and called the ambulance. The cuts were not life threatening, but Amy's behavior was bizarre. She acted as though this was something cute and mischievous that she had done. The next week Beth took an overdose of Midol and beer. She called the ambulance herself before losing consciousness and was admitted into a medical hospital, where she stayed for two weeks.

At this point, therapist and supervisor consulted the author to see if a paradoxical pretending technique could be used to solve the problem of Beth and Amy's recurrent self-destructive behavior. The author asked the therapist the following question: If one were to assume that the suicidal girls were protective of one of the parents, which parent would it be? Which parent were the girls most concerned about? The therapist answered that the girls were concerned about the mother, since the mother was tired, overworked, and unhappy in her marriage, even though she was much more attractive than the father. The author proposed that an appropriate intervention might be to have the mother pretend to be exhausted and miserable in the session and have the daughters pretend to reassure and comfort her. At home, in the evening, the mother would do the same thing and would try to deceive the girls so that they would not know whether she was pretending or really feeling that way. The girls would reassure and comfort the mother to make her feel better. In this way, the mother would be overtly asking for help and the girls would be overtly helping her. The girls would be able to help their mother in a more appropriate and playful way than by attempting suicide. The mother would be overtly put down in the hierarchy in relation to the daughters, and she would react against this situation by taking charge with appropriate motherly behavior—thus correcting the hierarchy. The hypotheses were that: the girls were a metaphor for the mother's depression and despair; the girls' plan was to help the mother by eliciting her concern for their suicidal behavior and getting her to focus on her situation as mother rather than as dejected, unhappy wife; and the helpfulness of the girls toward the mother resulted in a hierarchical reversal so that, in fact, the mother could not effectively help the daughters.

The supervisor in the case decided that it would be best to start the session with a review by the therapist of all the problems the family had brought to therapy and of everything that had been done during the therapy to solve those problems. If, in the discussion, the issue of the daughters' concern for the mother came up, the author would be called in behind the one-way mirror to supervise the pretending intervention and would continue to supervise the case from then on.

The parents and four daughters (one was away at college) were present at the session that began with the review the therapist had planned. Then the father was asked to read a suicide note by Beth that the mother had brought to the session. In the note, Beth said that her mother was "working her ass off to pay the fucking bills" and was "unhappy all the time" and that she, Beth, "worked my ass off in school to make only one person happy and that's my mother." When the father finished reading the note, the mother was teary, and Beth and Amy hid their faces under their hair. The therapist talked with them about the girls' concern for their mother. It was decided that there was enough evidence for this preoccupation, and the author was called in behind the one-way mirror to supervise. The pretending intervention began with the therapist asking the mother to pretend to be very tired and depressed, as she usually was at home, and for the rest of the family to watch to see if she did it well. At this request, Beth and Amy came out from under their hair for the first time in the interview and looked at the therapist and the mother with interest. The mother said it was difficult to pretend while sitting on a chair instead of lying down, so the therapist suggested that she could lie down on the floor and all the others could join her by also moving from their chairs to the floor. They did this with considerable giggling, and the mother lay on her side on the carpet, faintly muttering that she was tired. When asked if the mother's pretending was realistic, the father said that it was and that sometimes she would lie on the couch and sometimes on the bed. The older daughter Meg said that the mother usually covered herself with an afghan, and the therapist asked Amy to give her mother her jacket to use as a pretend afghan. The therapist encouraged the mother to pretend more realistically by saying that she felt like a little baby who was tired of all these children and all these responsibilities and that she just wanted to cuddle up and do nothing. In fact, these words described the way in which the mother often presented herself.

After a few minutes of pretending by the mother, the girls were asked to approach her and comfort and reassure her. Meg and Jo quickly sat next to her, patted her on the back, and asked her if there was anything she needed; but Beth and Amy remained shy and distant, despite numerous attempts by the therapist to encourage them to approach their mother in a helpful way. Finally, Beth went over to her and playfully said, "Get up, Mom. I have to sell the couch," and sat across the mother's legs. Then Amy got up, offered the mother some tea, and aimlessly wandered around the room pretending to get her a cup. The therapist suggested that all the girls should embrace and kiss the mother because she needed a great deal of love and caring. The girls embraced her affectionately, with Beth and Amy again being the last to do so.

While all this pretending and hugging was going on among the women in the family, the father had moved to a chair in the corner of the room and was sitting hunched over, with his head in his hand, a picture of total dejection. The author, supervising from behind the mirror, became concerned about his depressed attitude. This concern led to the thought that if the supervisor could be so worried, how much more worried his own daughters must be about seeing him in this dejected mood. Perhaps the intervention was wrong and the par-

ent that the daughters were trying to help in devious and self-
destructive ways was the father and not the mother. In fact, the
girls' suicide attempts had the quality of the despondent ges-
tures of an abandoned lover. Furthermore, what the suicide attempts accomplished was that the mother could not leave the
father while they were trying to save the lives of their daughters
—and this was April, the month in which the mother had said
she would leave. The girls were helping the father by keeping his
wife with him. But this helpfulness incapacitated the father and
prevented him from being either a father to the girls or a husband to the wife.

Acting on this hypothesis, the therapist was instructed
first to finish the previous directive by asking the father to also
embrace and comfort the wife, then to shift the focus to the
father and ask *him* now to pretend to be depressed and miserable. The father knelt on the floor and embraced his wife tenderly; the mother hugged him back and appeared pleased. The
therapist asked the father to sit down and pretend that he was
depressed and overwhelmed with financial problems, ashamed
that his wife had to work, and very worried about the troubles
that his daughters were giving him. The father said that that
would take no pretending. In fact, the father had used these
very words in the past to describe his situation. He proceeded
to pretend by sitting in the chair for a few minutes looking dejected, just as he had looked for most of the session. Then the
girls were asked to comfort the father. They all jumped up immediately and stood in line to hug him and kiss him, Beth and
Amy equally or perhaps even more eagerly than the other two
sisters. The therapist asked the father whether he would like to
have the girls do this a second time; he said yes, and the girls
jumped up once more with great enthusiasm. The reaction from
the girls indicated that the hypothesis probably was correct and
that the girls were very interested in helping the father. The
girls' cooperation with the directive to pretend to comfort the
father was an indication that the metaphor had been understood and the therapy was on the right track. In contrast, they
had been extremely reluctant to pretend to comfort the mother. If the children refuse to participate in a pretending tech-

nique, the therapist has probably made a mistake and misunderstood the metaphor in the children's symptomatic behavior. In this case, the girls also were probably reluctant to comfort the mother because, if they were attempting suicide to keep her at home, they had to feel resentful toward the mother for requiring from them such extreme, destructive behavior.

The mother was then asked to approach the husband and embrace him. She responded as if she had to go out of her way to establish in front of everyone that she had a special position as the wife and that the husband belonged to her. She slowly strutted toward him, sat on his lap, and talked about their quiet moments in the kitchen while she hugged and kissed him.

The therapist instructed the parents to each perform this pretending at home several times every evening that week, just as they had done in the session, emphasizing that sometimes they would really be feeling tired and depressed and at other times they would be just pretending, but they would do it in such a way that the girls would not know when they were pretending. The girls would comfort each parent in the same ways as they had in the session, and they would also each plan a small surprise for each parent that week.

The next interview was held one week later. The family lived an hour and a half away, and when the mother was getting ready to leave for the session with three of the daughters, she discovered that her car would not start. The father was on the other side of town with Amy and the nine-year-old son, whom he was bringing to the session. There was no time for the father to pick up the rest of the family, so he came alone with the two children. He looked happy and optimistic and reported that, even though there had been no pretending, everybody in the family had hugged and kissed each other very frequently that week and the whole atmosphere of the house had changed. The girls had gone out of their way to be nice to each other, to their brother, and to the parents. Beth, whose suicide note had been read in the previous session, had left another note for the father, apologizing for having difficulty in being affectionate to the parents as had been required in the session. The father had spoken with her and told her that it was not her fault but his, because he had never given any of the children the kind of affection that a child needs in its early years. This was the first time the therapist had heard that the father felt guilty and neglectful, but she did not comment on his statement. This kind of insight often follows rapid change in therapy, and it is best to accept it respectfully and move on. The father said that from now on he would change and devote himself 100 percent to taking care of his family.

The therapist told the father that the same directive about pretending would carry over for the next week since half the family was not present, and she asked him to explain the instructions to his son, who had not been at the previous session. The father carefully explained the instructions without omitting anything. He then pretended once more to be depressed, and Amy and the boy comforted him. In this way they would remember what to do at home.

Amy reported that the girls had solved one other serious problem at home. The family had only one bathroom, and all four girls needed to wash their hair every morning before going to school or they would refuse to go. The only hair dryer the family owned was in the one bathroom, so every morning a battle for the bathroom took place. The girls had solved the problem that week by organizing a shifting schedule in which they would take turns using the bathroom starting at six o'clock in the morning. This solution had made for a better feeling between the sisters.

The session ended with the therapist congratulating the father for the changes he had brought about in his family. The father was pleased and said that he now knew what he had to do and would do it. He would devote himself "100 percent full time to his family."

Therapist and supervisor planned that the next session would be the last. Once the father had expressed that he would solve the problem, the therapist had to give him the chance to do so and let him go. His confidence indicated that the girls no longer needed to protect him, and it would have been an error to undermine this confidence in any way.

The next session was a week later, and the whole family

was present. Everybody was happy. There had been no pretending, but the children had done little things for the parents,
such as giving them breakfast in bed, tea, hugs, and surprises.
They were all getting along well. The therapist congratulated
both parents and asked them how they could ensure the continuity of change. The father answered that he would do so by
demonstrating affection to the children and spending time with
them and that the children needed to continue being affectionate to each other and to the mother. That day was the parents'
wedding anniversary, and the therapist took the opportunity to
bring them closer together. Each was asked to express his or her
love to the other, which they did, and they kissed romantically,
to the giggles and applause of all the children.

A follow-up a year later showed that all was well with the
family; the father had remodeled the house and was very proud
of his wife and daughters. A second follow-up three years later
showed that the girls were still symptom free and the parents
were together.

To summarize the case, the girls' suicide attempts were
expressing their own despair and that of the father. The command aspect of the self-destructive behavior was to order the
mother to take care of them and not to leave them and,
therefore, not to leave the father. The daughters' request for
the mother's caring presence was conveyed through self-destructive behavior and was a metaphor for the father's need for the
mother. Because the parents' attention was focused on the
girls, the father had never had to overtly express his wish for
the mother not to leave him: the girls expressed it for him.
The girls' plan was to prevent the mother from leaving, since
she was needed to take care of two suicidal daughters. This
helpfulness toward the father, however, created a worse problem than it was intended to solve, preventing the parents from
coming together in joy and with a focus on their own relationship rather than on the girls. The daughters appeared helpless
because of their suicidal behavior, yet they were powerful as unfortunate helpers to the parents.

The therapeutic strategy was to arrange for each parent
to overtly appear helpless by pretending depression rather than

covertly requesting help as they had been doing. The daughters would overtly help them by demonstrating affection rather than by behaving suicidally. Both parents then could spontaneously imitate the daughters' behavior and demonstrate affection toward each other. The father reacted against being in an inferior position when he pretended depression and helplessness. He took charge of the girls in appropriate, caring, paternal ways, and the hierarchy in the family was corrected not only in terms of authority but also in terms of affect. Without the girls' interference, the parents could resolve their difficulties with each other in their own ways and come together in good feeling.

2

*Discovering
the Source
of the Conflict*

The previous chapter presented a model for understanding a problem brought to therapy. This model included the concept of metaphorical sequences of interaction, in which the interchange between persons A and B is a metaphor and replaces the interaction between persons A and C. Relationships also can be metaphorical in ways other than those already mentioned—ways that preserve relationships at great cost to the participants. A conflictual interaction between a parent and a child may be a metaphor for and replace the conflictual interaction between the parent and another child. One sibling then may be able to grow and develop at the cost of the other sibling, who becomes intensely involved in a cross-generational conflict with the parent. Inasmuch as the three persons involved are engaged in conflicting interactions that are metaphorical for other conflicts, the three will remain attached to each other. Conflicts that are expressed metaphorically cannot be directly addressed and resolved. Other relationships will suffer.

In a similar way, persons A and B may argue about their relationship with person C. A might say that B is cruel and rejecting toward C, and B might say that A is too fond of C, too demanding of B, and unrealistic about both relationships. At a certain point, A and B may stop arguing about C and argue instead about issue X in their relationship. A might say that B is too demanding of A, is too concerned about X, and has unrealistic expectations. B might say that A is cruel and rejecting toward B and indifferent about issue X. The interaction of A and B about X would have become a metaphor for and replaced the interactions of A and B about C. The way A behaves toward B in relation to X will be similar to the way that B relates to C in relation to A. However, although there are advantages to the flexibility that derives from the possibility of shifting from one issue to another, neither conflict will be resolved. It is the very possibility of shifting to a metaphorical level that precludes the resolution of the problem.

Renegotiating Contracts

Tacit agreements between participants about the benefits accrued from an involvement are characteristic of ongoing relationships. Jackson (Lederer and Jackson, 1968) refers to this process in marriage as the "marital quid pro quo," postulating that for a marriage to be satisfying to both parties there must be an egalitarian distribution of benefits accrued to each from the relationship. That is, A will do something for B if B does something for A. If A does much more for B than B does for A, the continuity of the relationship is threatened. The concept of quid pro quo also is applicable to relationships other than marriage. Involvements between parents and children, between siblings, and between friends also include tacit agreements about the benefits that must accrue to each party. When these expectations are not met within a relationship, the relationship is in trouble.

It follows logically from these concepts that when couples or families are having difficulty, all that is necessary to solve the problem is to negotiate a new contract that is more favorable to all involved so that benefits will be more equally distributed. However, the nature of problems presented to therapy is such that the participants are involved in involuntary, helpless behavior that cannot be changed through reasonable negotiation. For example, if a husband and wife consult because the wife is agoraphobic and the therapist approaches the problem with the idea of attempting to renegotiate a quid pro quo in reasonable ways, the following situation could develop. The therapist might ask the husband what he would like to obtain from the relationship with his wife. The husband would say that he would like to go out with her, go to the movies, go to a restaurant, visit relatives, go shopping, or engage in some other similar activity. In this way he would have a wife that would be like other men's wives, and he would be happy with his marriage. Then the therapist might ask the wife what she wants from the relationship with her husband. The wife would answer that she wants the same thing that her husband wants. She would like to go out with him, visit friends, go to the movies, or the like, but no matter how much she wants this, she cannot do it; she is helpless to change behavior that to her is involuntary. The therapist is unable to negotiate a better quid pro quo between the couple: husband and wife are in agreement, but they are helpless to change. The problem must be tackled in indirect ways and not through reasonable negotiations.

Hierarchy and Power

The irrational, involuntary aspect of a relationship is more clearly apparent in a marriage than in most other relationships. However, it is present in all kinds of involvements in which tacit contracts are negotiated over time by the participants, who can only be led to renegotiation through indirect means. The idea that there is a tacit contract for the distribution of benefits in an ongoing relationship is related to issues of hierarchy and power. The magnitude of importance of the benefits obtained defines a position of power or weakness. The participant who is in a position of providing benefits that are necessary for the survival and well being of others is in a position superior to that of the participants who cannot provide such benefits and who are dependent on obtaining them from others. Parents are in a position superior to that of their children in that the benefits they derive from their children's love and concern are of a different order and magnitude from those they provide to the children in terms of the children's survival and well being. In fact, the family originated for the purpose of caring for the young, and hierarchical differences between the generations have been clear throughout the history of the family. It can be argued that the helpless baby who cries for attention has more power over the mother than the mother has over the baby, and it certainly has more power than do the older siblings. Undoubtedly, a baby can derive power over the family from helpless crying, but this power is minimal compared to the family's power to neglect, harm, or lovingly care for the baby.

The benefits parents and children obtain from their relationship are repeatedly renegotiated as children grow older and the family constellation varies. This renegotiation may involve metaphorical sequences. For example, father and older son may be locked in a struggle that escalates, creating conflicts of loyalty among other family members. At a certain point, father and younger son may develop a conflict that, as it increases in magnitude, will ensure equality between the brothers, prevent the conflict between father and older son from escalating further, and stabilize the family, preserving the quid pro quo. The children's ability to create or sustain conflicts that express and replace other conflicts in the family is a source of power that threatens the hierarchical stability of the system. In the same way, when the distribution of benefits in a marriage is altered and the couple struggles to reestablish a quid pro quo, the distribution of power and responsibility and the hierarchical organization of the couple are threatened.

Within this framework for understanding relationships, the therapist's task is to change metaphors, arrange for a redistribution of benefits, and renegotiate contracts. All this must be accomplished against the background of the grim, pessimistic view of life usually presented to a therapist by those who have attempted to solve their own problems and failed. A sense of humor in viewing the problem and humorous techniques for resolving it are the saving grace for therapists who must attempt, day after day, to raise people from a negative view of sordid problems to an optimistic view where problems are solvable.

When the unit of therapy is the family and not the individual, paradoxical techniques can be used in a variety of ways. Rather than relying on prescribing the symptom to the person with the presenting problem, the therapist has other possible alternatives. For example, the therapist can prescribe the symptom with a small modification of the context. Who has the symptom, where, when, how, and with whom can be changed. The two case examples that follow illustrate this approach.* In the first, who had the symptom was changed. In the second, a change was made in terms of when, where, and how the problem would occur. In both cases, humor was used to change metaphors, redistribute benefits, and renegotiate contracts.

The Life Ruiner

A twenty-one-year-old youth was referred for court-ordered therapy. During the previous few years, he had been charged several times with stealing, possession of drugs, and drunken driving. He had left home at age twenty and was living with some young people when he became depressed and admitted himself to a psychiatric ward, where he was described as presenting bizarre communication and disturbed thinking. After a few weeks, he was discharged and soon after was arrested once more for drunken driving. At the time, he was living at home with his parents, who were working-class people, his twenty-six-year-old brother, Frank, who was a schoolteacher with a master's degree in education, and his twenty-three-year-old sister, Ann, who was a cashier at a store.

The young man, Tommy, came to the first therapy session with his parents and his siblings. The therapist used a direct approach in this first session (in which the supervisor behind the one-way mirror was not the author). The parents were put in charge of the young man, and they agreed on rules for him and

*The therapists in these cases were Carol Waser, M.A., and Vicki Karlin, M.S.W.

consequences if the rules were not followed. The parents' rules coincided with those of the court: no drugs, no alcohol, no lying around the house doing nothing. The parents also agreed that he should begin looking for a job.

The family returned the following week (to the first session supervised by the author), and the parents reported that there had been no change. Tommy had spent the week lying in bed smoking and drinking beer and had not been out to look for a job. The supervisor noticed that in this family not only Tommy but also his two adult siblings were still living at home and, even though they had good jobs, they did not contribute to the household. Since this is an unusual arrangement for an American working-class family, it was thought that a discussion of the circumstances might clarify some important issues. Therapist and supervisor decided that the therapist should inquire about how much it cost the parents to support these three adult children and what alternative uses they could find for that money. This discussion would help therapist and supervisor understand the hierarchy, the distribution of benefits, and the metaphors in the family, and it would lead to the development of a strategy for change.

The parents discussed their expenses, wrote down their calculations, and concluded that supporting their three adult children cost them $1,200 per month. The therapist emphasized that part of this money was used to support habits the parents did not wish to support. She said, referring to Tommy, "So $4.00 a day you give him to help support his nicotine habit, his alcohol habit, and possibly his drug habit."

"Why bring in a possible drug habit?" interrupted Tommy, looking tough in his motorcycle-gang-style jacket.

"But we're not giving it to him to support it," said the mother. "We're giving it to him because if we didn't give it to him I don't know how he would walk around. He couldn't hitchhike down to the unemployment office on that day or wherever he has to go."

"I'd rather he had money than go try to steal it from someone or someplace," contributed the father.

The therapist said, "So he blackmails you into giving him money to support his habit with the threat of stealing."

"No, not threat of; he has done it before," corrected the father. "I'd rather we gave him some money than have him possibly go out and try to steal it from somebody or someplace."

"And assume the responsibility yourselves for helping support his nicotine habit and his alcohol habit," continued the therapist. "This $1,200 here that you're putting out each month to support your children, I'd like you to think a minute, to take a little fantasy trip. What could you do, the two of you together, with $1,200 a month to spend as you would want to?"

"Don't talk to me, talk to her," said the father, pointing to his wife, "because I have said that to her. How long and how much?"

"Talk together a minute. Have you ever taken a trip?"

"Oh, yes, we did!" smiled the mother.

"We cancelled one because of him," said the father, pointing at Tommy.

"We cancelled one on February 19th to the 25th, but last spring we went to the Bahamas, and before that we went to Jamaica. We did cancel a trip February 19th to the 25th to Puerto Rico," said the mother, obviously interested in the subject.

"So you missed a trip to Puerto Rico."

"Not because of money, because of his situation," said the father, once again pointing at Tommy.

"Because of me," muttered Tommy, as if he were making an accusation.

"But there can be other trips," said the mother.

"All because of me," continued Tommy, with great resentment in his voice. "Because of me, right? Yeah, all the trips that they plan they can't do because of me, because I'm in the house."

At this point in the interview, the supervisor began to wonder why Tommy was so resentful and why he was protesting so much that he was the cause of the parents' troubles. Hoping to provoke him further and in that way elicit more information, the supervisor instructed the therapist to continue joining the parents in the conversation about their trips and to praise them for their imagination and fun-loving nature. In fact, these parents were quite serious, rigid people, and it was hoped that in this way some playful aspect of their character would be elic-

ited. A session conducted in a playful way sets a good framework for an indirect approach. The supervisor did not yet know
what the therapeutic strategy would be and was waiting for a
better understanding of the family before designing a plan. The
therapist said, "I have to apologize to you for assuming that
you were just an ordinary, boring, hard-working couple."

"Okay," said the father.

"You know what you are really is . . ."

"Suckers," interrupted the father.

"No, people who are fun loving. I don't know many people who have planned a trip to Jamaica, been to the Bahamas,
planned a trip to Puerto Rico. I think that's just wonderful.
You have imagination, you have plans, you have things that you
want to do together. If you had this $1,200 a month to spend
as you would wish, how would you spend it?"

"Probably on our kids," said the father, with resignation.

"That's exactly right," emphasized the mother. "We'd
probably spend it on our children."

"What would you tell your wife that you would like to
do? Would you tell her, Mr. Mitchell?"

"I'm trying. It was at my insistence to go that we went
on a winter vacation to Jamaica."

"I think you're really fortunate to have a husband like
this."

"I am, I am," said the mother, while the husband laughed.

"Oh, my goodness, to be wanting to provide this kind of
thing for the two of you. That $12 thousand a year, just as a
fantasy, fantasy island, where would you take your wife, what
would you do with your wife if you had that money? Twelve
thousand dollars."

"I'd try to take her to Jamaica and trade her off for two
twenty-five-year-olds." He laughed, and the mother joined him in
the laughter.

"But aren't we getting off the subject?"

"Stay on the subject," said Tommy. "I like it, I'm getting into it."

"It's off of you, what's why," answered the father, with
an accusatory finger once more pointed at Tommy.

"I'm getting into it," said Tommy. "All you care about—Santa Monica, San Francisco, California—keep on going. You got half an hour more to go. They're only worried about their problem, they're not worried about my problem."

Tommy expressed his resentment once more. This resentment was incongruous with his position in the family as a delinquent son. It is as if he resented some sacrifice that he was making for his family that he could not make explicit and that his parents did not appreciate. Hoping to gain a better understanding of the reasons for this resentment, the supervisor instructed the therapist to explore the emotional relationship between the parents and the three children and to phrase the inquiry as a competition between the siblings so as to elicit information on what part the brother and sister played in the situation. The therapist addressed the three siblings, "Whom does your dad love the most of the three of you?"

"His wife," replied Tommy.

"And of his children, whom does he love?"

"I don't know about that, I couldn't care less," answered Tommy.

"I just feel I've never lived up to the expectations set on me," said Frank, with anxiety in his voice. "I've just never been quite good enough."

"Which of you has the most dramatic clashes with your dad?"

"Hum. Hum. Who's the session for? Mostly me," said Tommy, almost boastfully.

"The two of you agree? Does Tommy have the most dramatic clashes with your dad?"

Frank answered, "It used to be me, and then Tom took my place when I grew a little bit older. But we still have our times."

"So it was you, and then your brother took over that role."

"But I haven't completely abandoned it," said Frank.

The supervisor began to suspect that perhaps Frank was telling the truth. It could be that the older brother had had conflicts with the father that had escalated over time until they had become intolerable to the family because of the threat of total alienation between father and son or because the mother sided with Frank against the father and the marriage was threatened. It could be that, as the conflict between the father and Frank became intolerable, Tommy began to have difficulties and cause trouble and in this way replaced Frank in the conflict with the father. Tommy's behavior was so extreme that the mother could not side with him against the father, so marital harmony was preserved. However, although Tommy was helpful to his brother in getting him off the spot by calling the father's anger upon himself, his way of helping was so disruptive to the family that it prevented Frank and the father from facing their conflicts and resolving them.

"And who has the most dramatic clashes with your mother?" asked the therapist.

"I guess it goes for me, too," said Tommy. "Yeah, if it ain't one, it's the other. If it ain't one, it's the other one."

"So you're the dramatic clasher of the kids."

"Yeah. Because of what happened to my exciting life. It all comes, it all boils down to me. I'm the life ruiner. The number one life ruiner. I guess they come in second and third," said Tommy, gesturing toward his brother and sister.

Tommy insisted so much that he was "the number one life ruiner" that it was difficult not to think of him as a metaphor for someone else: his brother. Otherwise, he would not have protested so much. The strategy for the therapy followed logically. If the conflict between Tommy and the father was a metaphor for and replaced the conflict between Frank and the father, then the goal of the therapy should be to take the conflict back to where it originated—between the father and Frank —and to resolve it so that Tommy could be freed from replacing his brother and instead could occupy himself with improving his own life. This goal could be accomplished in three stages.

In the first stage, a paradoxical intervention would be used. The same behavior, defined so well by Tommy in his statement, "I'm the life ruiner," would be prescribed, with a small modification of the context. The family would still have a life ruiner, but *who* would be the life ruiner would change. Based on a basic principle of American culture—the idea of taking turns democratically in every activity—the therapist would suggest that the siblings take turns at being the life ruiner, so that there would be a different life ruiner every week. Then Tommy would not have to be the life ruiner all the time, and the parents would know what to expect.

The second stage would consist of the reaction of the three siblings against the therapist's directive and their refusal to deliberately take the position of life ruiner, including Tommy, who would begin to behave normally. In the third stage, with Tommy no longer a metaphor for his brother, the conflict between the father and Frank would emerge and it would become possible to resolve it. Unpredictably, the family went through these three stages in three sessions.

The therapist ended the first session by giving the paradoxical prescription, "Before we adjourn and set our time for next week, I'd like the three of you young people to agree on who's going to be the life ruiner for this week, so your folks will be forewarned."

"Well, I can answer that," said Tommy. "Until I get a job, I'll be the life ruiner. Let's put it that way."

"Come to an agreement. You've got to have the agreement of your brother and your sister."

"They probably agree too."

"I don't understand the question," said Frank.

"Who's going to be the life ruiner, the disrupter, for the week?" answered the therapist.

"The dog," said Ann.

"It's been me ever since, so I can't stop now, or I'll . . . ," said Tommy.

This was a very insightful comment from Tommy. It was quite true that he could not stop. Once a metaphorical sequence of interaction is established in a family, it is maintained by all and difficult to change.

"Why . . ." interrupted Ann, a plain-looking girl who was not as verbal or as attractive as her brothers.

"Talk to your brother and your sister and come to an agreement."

"Wait a minute," said Ann.

"Are you saying that to try to get us to . . . ," began Frank, but he was interrupted by Ann: "No, I disagree." ". . . to behave better this week?" finished Frank.

"Why are you thinking next week there's going to be a life ruiner?" said Ann. "Why can't we think positive? Why can't the problem sort of fade out? Why? Huh? Do you have an answer?"

"Don't you go day by day?" said Tommy.

"I think it would be wonderful if things would be positive and smooth, and I think that would be just wonderful," answered the therapist. "But that's not the way it has been, and I think the likelihood of that happening this week is not very great. And your father's coming up in years, he's not getting any younger, and I think it would be a service to him so that he would be forewarned about who's going to cause the trouble this week. But we need to decide before we can disband who's going to be the ruiner, the life ruiner for the week. The three of you need to agree on who it's going to be."

"I'll do it this week," volunteered Frank. "What do you want me to do?"

"That will be up to you. Is that agreeable with your brother and your sister, however, that you assume the role for the week? Is that okay with you, Tom?"

"Yeah," said Tommy.

"How about with you, Ann?"

"What are we getting at, though? Why? Explain," said Ann. "Do we have to have somebody to do something every week?"

"Well, it is necessary that your parents and that your father be forewarned as to who's going to cause the trouble this week so that he'll be prepared and able to deal with it and not be shocked."

"No, you don't have this," said Tommy emphatically. "It's me, because before the week's over something will crop up, to me. I mean if it ain't taking out the trash, cutting grass, trimming, something'll crop up. It ain't you. You and Ann are never no life ruiners. It's number one, that's who it is, I think. Me."

It was clear that Tommy was reluctant to give up his position.

"Well, you guys have to agree before we can end this."

"You can have it back next week," said Frank to Tommy. "I'll take it this week, then you'll have it back next week."

"So you're going to try to ruin, to have something ruin their life?" Tommy asked Frank.

"Is it contagious, Frank?" inquired Ann.

"It's not, it's not . . . ," said Tommy.

"I didn't get my shots," commented Ann looking at her arms.

"It's not a schoolteacher to ruin the life. It's a person that's unemployed," argued Tommy.

"It doesn't have to be," answered the father.

"Oh yeah it does. Who was the life ruiner for last week?" said Tommy.

"Last week is last week," said the therapist. "We're talking about the week coming up. I need an agreement among the three of you."

"I'll be proud to take that. I'll be proud to take that," insisted Tommy.

"If he wants to," said Frank.

"You all agree, it's not for me to decide," said the therapist.

"Unless Ann wants to take it. Now I come to think of it, it might not be me," said Tommy, looking at Ann.

"I have to see how my schedule is first," answered Ann.

"I try to teach them to be decisive," said the father, "to make that choice, right or wrong, but at least make it."

The conversation about who was going to be the life ruiner was rather bizarre, but this statement by the father, encouraging his children to make the decision to be a life ruiner, was particularly curious.

"And they need to make that decision today," said the therapist, "to be decisive. He was just suggesting that maybe he didn't want to do it after all."

"Yeah, something might happen with Ann," said Tommy. "I got a little ESP something might happen, so let's pick straws or something, get it over with."

"I think the two of you need to discuss it, the three of you."

"You be it, Frank, you're better," said Ann.

"Yeah, well that's what I said originally. I'll do it. I don't know why everyone was trying to talk me out of it. I said I'd do it at the beginning. So it's settled."

"So it's settled," agreed Tommy.

"Are you in agreement on it?" asked the therapist.

"Yeah, I'll take it next week, then," said Tommy.

"All right, you're agreeing that Frank will be the ruiner. Ann, are you in agreement? And Frank, you're it." The therapist rose from her chair. "Okay, I shall see you next week at 9:15."

Tommy had reluctantly relinquished his position for one week.

One week later, the therapist started the session by asking Frank, "So how was the life ruiner this week? What did you do?"

"I just did what I normally do."

"And what was that?"

"You mean that ruined the family?"

"How did you ruin the lives of the family this week?"

"Um, well, going back to what we said last week, not paying rent. Just freeloading, basically."

"Okay, how about you, Tom? What did you think about your brother fulfilling the task this week of being the ruiner?"

"I didn't think nothing of it."

"Well, what did you see him doing?"

"Nothing I could see, cause I was working from 4 to 9 P.M. So I couldn't see."

The change was more rapid than either therapist or supervisor had expected. One week after Frank volunteered to take the position of life ruiner, Tommy had a job. It would have been a mistake, however, for the therapist to show that she was pleased or to become interested in Tommy's job at the time when she should have been inquiring about how Frank fulfilled his task. So the therapist continued to talk about the older brother and returned later to the subject of Tommy's job.

"How about you, Mrs. Mitchell? What did you observe this week in terms of your older son carrying out his task?"

"I couldn't see that he specifically ruined anything."

"How about you, Mr. Mitchell? He didn't seem to carry it through from your point of view either?"

"You mean you were actually expecting him to do something?"

"Oh, I sure did. Sure."

"No," said the father with a little laugh.

The therapist turned to Tommy, "You're working?"

"Uhum. Second day at the job."

"What are you doing?"

"Gas station job."

"Tell me about how you got the job."

"From a friend I used to go out at night with."

"And how often do you work?"

"Monday, Wednesday, and Saturday, until I get on the schedule."

"And it's what? You said four to nine?"

"Uhum. It's seven to three o'clock on Saturdays."

After some discussion of how Frank had failed to be the life ruiner that week, the therapist said, "Who's going to be the life ruiner for the next two-week period? Because I won't be seeing you again for two weeks, so we need to talk about that."

"I think you ought to do it, Ann," said the father.

"I'd like the three of you to come to an agreement in the way that you did last week. I thought you handled the discussion very well, because it took a lot of negotiating, and I'd like the three of you to do that."

"Our basic purpose in being here is for Tom, and I think we have to examine other members of the family on our way to examining him, so I think she should go next," said Frank, pointing to Ann.

"Does there have to be a life ruiner every week?" asked Tommy.

"For a while," said the therapist.

"For a while?" repeated Tommy.

"Uh huh."

"That just brings up grief and all that, don't it?"

"Your brother didn't even carry out the task last week. I'm hoping the next one will do a better job."

"Oh, I can carry it out, I can carry it out. I could probably do three or four things to be yelled at for," said Tommy. "But, you know, I just don't want to hear it!"

"So it sounds like you don't particularly want to volunteer for that task," replied the therapist.

"No, I don't particularly want to volunteer for nothing, no more now, because I'm twenty-one years old and I know about what, about what he's gonna say if I did something wrong about some certain thing."

"Yeah, I agree with that," interjected Frank.

"And I know about what kind of attitude he's gonna put towards me in telling me it. So I've given up on life ruining as a whole way," said Tommy emphatically.

This is the statement the therapist was looking for, so she provoked him to make him stick to his position: "You know, you don't even look tough enough to me to be a sustained full-time life ruiner. You look too kind. You have too kind a face."

"No," said Tommy.

"You really don't look like you could carry it off that well," insisted the therapist.

"Oh, I can carry it off now," boasted Tommy.

"No, I don't know. Now your sister looks a lot tougher to me. I bet she could pull it off."

"I could have, I could have something done. We could come back here two weeks from now and we could probably have about four or five things I've done wrong deliberately, you know, to make it that way," said Tommy. "If you want a life ruiner, I'll make it that way."

Tommy not only refused to continue in his old ways but he admitted that his behavior was deliberate and not involuntary and symptomatic. This admission is what the therapist was after, because if Tommy could produce the behavior deliberately, then he could also not produce it deliberately.

Frank said, "I don't think he should be it this coming week, though. There's been too much attention on him. We need to get it off on another family member."

"It certainly is important during this period for one of the children to assume this role so that it won't be too much of a shock for your parents," said the therapist, "so they know what to expect, although I must say you didn't carry it through in the way I expected. I'm going to expect a more sustained effort from the person who volunteers for the coming period. If you volunteer, then that person will be very alert to what the other two of you are thinking would be an appropriate way to carry it out, although I suspect that each of you has a fair amount of creativity to design a life-ruining process which would be pretty effective, I think. But you have to be willing to carry the task out."

"Well, now that I know a little bit more about how to do it," volunteered Frank, "I'll try it again for another week."

"Let me get this straight," said the father. "You're actually wanting one of those to assume the role of an agitator."

"Uh hum."

"And I'm supposed to sit idly back."

"Oh, I didn't say that, no," said the therapist. "The purpose is that this is what's going on all the time anyway. And if we designate one of the children as a life ruiner for a designated period, then the other two are free of that for that time and can get on with their lives." She turned to the mother, "I would assume that you would prefer that there not be a young person, one young person, who is causing disruption and upsetting the household in the way we've been talking."

"Well, I know you're getting at a point to see, you know, to have someone take that role, you know," answered the mother.

"But as a mother I would assume that you would want it to be peaceful and that there wouldn't be any life ruiners at all."

"Well, I guess every mother would want that . . . eventually."

"And wanting that is one thing, but if it can't be, the second choice would be to have one life ruiner rather than three."

"Yes, that's right."

"And that's why we're focusing on that."

The father said, "I would rather there be not a life ruiner

but a life brightener. This week I am going to totally concentrate on not bringing any more problems or thinking them out or doing them myself."

The father was very much of a grouch and played a large part in maintaining whatever conflicts were going on in the family. His promise to be a life brightener was as important to the therapy as Tommy's statement that he would no longer be the life ruiner. The three siblings discussed who would be the life ruiner in the next two weeks and did not reach agreement. So the therapist asked the parents to decide who it would be. The father immediately pointed at the mother, and the therapist quickly clarified that she meant which of the children would be the life ruiner. It was better to avoid any focus on marital difficulties until Tommy's problem was solved. Then, as metaphors in the family changed, it could well be that the marital problem would be resolved without an intervention by the therapist.

The father pointed to Ann and said, "I nominate her."

"You and your wife must agree, Mr. Mitchell," said the therapist.

"Well, I guess I would think it would be Ann this week," said the mother.

It could be that just as Tommy was a convenient metaphor to avoid conflicts between Frank and the father, Ann was a convenient metaphor to avoid conflicts between the mother and the father. The father had originally pointed at the mother as the life ruiner and then both parents singled out Ann. The therapist and the family stood up to leave and Ann rushed out of the room ahead of them, with tears in her eyes.

In the third session, it was immediately apparent that the family was in some sort of crisis. The mother, who had always before sat next to the father, was sitting next to Frank and was obviously upset. The father related that at the end of the last session Ann had refused to get into the father's car and had walked home instead, even though it meant an hour and a half walk. Apparently, she resented the fact that her parents had selected her to be the life ruiner.

"So you took the task far more seriously than your brother

Frank did. Immediately upon leaving the session, you took charge and did what you were asked. Did you do more things?" asked the therapist.

"You're saying took charge. I disagree," said the father. "She was upset. She did not take that task seriously. None of us did. Only upon your insistence that one of them take this role . . ."

"Well, now that they've taken all of these roles," said the mother, "do they have to keep taking them or can that be just, you know, cancelled out? That part of it? I mean, it's accomplished what it was intended to accomplish, whatever that was."

"What happened during the week? What did you do, Ann, to carry out the task?"

"Nothing wrong," said Ann.

"Well, I'm wondering, Mr. and Mrs. Mitchell, do you think that Tommy should have the assignment of being the life ruiner so that things are at least uncomfortable in a familiar way?"

"I don't think anybody should," said the father.

"I don't think anybody should have the specific task of life ruining," agreed the mother. "I think you should have another theory or some other procedure to follow other than that. I mean I don't think it should be designated to him. It should be along some other line of thought. We're more or less coming to help Tommy, and I mean he's, you know, the particular person under the court order to come, you know. And we don't have to make up something to ruin life."

As the mother insisted that the therapy was for Tommy, she pointed to Frank. The supervisor took this as an indication that some problem had erupted in relation to Frank. Perhaps the third stage of the therapy already had been reached and the conflict between the father and Frank would emerge. The therapist was directed to talk to Frank, to try to bring him out and get him to say what was happening with him.

"What do you think about that, Frank? Do you think that your parents should give the assignment of life ruiner to Tommy in order to keep things more stable?"

"Well, I agree with my mother," answered Frank. "That's

why we're here is to help him, so we should be concentrating our efforts on helping him.''

"So what you all are saying is that you're here to help him, that he has been the life ruiner. That's a term that he coined the first session that we were here. And you're saying then that perhaps it would be the most appropriate to go ahead and let him continue to assume that role. What do you think of it, Tommy? Are you willing to continue to assume that responsibility of being life ruiner so that the family will have some kind of predictability, so that they will know what to expect? Do you think your brother and sister want to help you out now?''

"Huh? Help me out life ruining?'' said Tommy. "They don't need to do that. I'm willing. I'm 100 percent up to doing that. I can make it as miserable as I want, but I already know what's going to be said, I already know what the tone of voice is gonna be, so I don't do it.''

"You know, I fail to realize,'' said the father to the therapist, "when you're hearing him say this, why you don't come back and say 'Why do you persist in doing it? Why do you do it?' ''

"I think he does it in order to save his brother and sister. I think he does it so that they can get on with what they need to do, and it seems to me that if they were to assume part of the responsibility of being life ruiners, he might be able to stay out of jail. If he's a life ruiner only one week out of three, the probability of his ending up in jail is lessened by two thirds. So, did you have trouble giving up the life ruiner position for the week? Were you able to give it up for the week because we had assigned it to Ann?''

"Yeah,'' said Tommy.

"How was your week?''

"Huh?''

"How was your week? Did you do any life ruining this week?''

"I can't remember.''

Tommy hardly seemed to remember what the therapist was talking about. This was a sign that he had changed and his old problems might be behind him.

"Did anyone else observe? How was the week with Tommy?"

"He got a job," said Frank.

"He had a job last week. Do you have a different job this week?"

"No, the same job."

"Continuing to work. So I think that we can say that he has given up part of the job of being life ruiner because he's got a part-time job."

"He's doing fairly well. I've aged him a few years," said the father.

"He's given up part of it," said the therapist. "But this week he could have given up more of it if Ann had taken on the role of life ruiner for the whole week instead of just one day. If Ann had been the life ruiner for the whole week, he'd have a full-time job by now. And so the question I have for you, Frank, and for you, Ann, is . . ."

"No," said Ann.

"How can you help your brother? Are you willing to help your brother?"

"I am not gonna be that person this week," said Ann. "No."

"Ann and Frank, will the two of you talk about this?"

"I cannot walk home now because it is a little bit later," said Ann. "If I want to, I can get up and leave. I'm not gonna do it."

"Frank, would you talk to your sister for a minute about how you and she can be of help to your brother, Tommy?"

"Well, I've taken my problems that I've contributed to the family and I'm moving out," said Frank. The mother squirmed in her chair, picked up her umbrella, and sat on it, laughing nervously. "The pain that I caused my parents will be eliminated," continued Frank. "I'm going—moving out on my own to develop more responsibility, into a situation where I have to pay rent. So that alleviates some of the problem they have with me."

Finally, Frank had said it. The crisis in the family was that he was moving out.

"So he won't be here for the life ruiner," said the mother, agitated.

"I'm not saying that what you should do is the same thing," said Frank to his brother and sister.

"He won't be here any more," said the mother to the therapist.

"But I'm taking the lead as the oldest," continued Frank.

"You're abandoning your brother?" said the therapist.

"I don't really call it abandoning," answered Frank.

"Abandoning the parents," said Tommy.

" 'Cause I think he knows I care about him," continued Frank. "I'm not abandoning my parents, I'm not abandoning my family, but I have a life of my own to live. I'm twenty-seven years old, and I need to develop some responsibility."

"When will you be moving out?" asked the therapist.

"Today and tomorrow."

"Oh, it's immediate."

"Yes, it's instant," said the mother, with great anxiety.

"It's a two-way process. There's no bitterness or anything, I'm just . . . It's just kind of reached a certain level where I don't feel like I can contribute any more to helping the situation."

The mother's anxiety was as great as if Frank were moving to another country. In fact, he was moving only a few blocks away, to a house that he would share with some young people that the mother knew and of whom she approved. The conversation continued with some discussion about Frank's living arrangements, and then Frank complained about not feeling appreciated by his father.

"I hardly get any compliments from you, ever," he said. "The attention I get from you is when I do something wrong, and I've gotten plenty of that for twenty-seven years."

Whatever the conflict was between Frank and the father, it was now coming to a head. There was an extreme atmosphere of tension and of painful resentment between them. In an attempt to improve the feeling between father and son, the supervisor suggested that the therapist ask the parents to give a blessing to their son who was preparing to leave home. This ritual is often effective in creating a benevolent atmosphere while emphasizing the appropriateness of the separation.

"You know, when a young person leaves home, it's important that he leave with the blessing of his parents," said the therapist. "And I would like for us to do that here in this room now. It would be appropriate for him to hear a blessing from his father and from his mother, to hear a compliment of something that he's done well, and your blessing and your wishing him well as he leaves."

Ann stood up suddenly and stomped out of the room, saying: "Goodbye to you and you and you and you."

The idea of the blessing from the parents, instead of alleviating the tension, increased it. Ann's departure was probably an attempt to call attention to herself and distract from the conflict with Frank; in this way, she assumed what had previously been Tommy's position in the family. This effect would have been accomplished if the therapist or the family had gone after her. It was important to continue the session without allowing her to be helpful in this way. From another point of view, it was a good sign with respect to Ann that, when she did not like the family situation, she could leave and extricate herself from the conflict.

"Very good. She's really taking it on very well," commented the therapist, referring to Ann.

"Well, Frank, you know I give you all the encouragement I can," said the mother. "You know I have in the past and I know you're doing the right thing by going down there. I know everything will work out okay."

"And a compliment of something that has pleased you."

"You've gotten commendations, I've been down to the school, from your supervisor, Mrs. Robins."

"You don't really have to say all these things, because you've conveyed them all your life," said Frank.

"So I haven't," interjected the father bitterly. "I'm getting ready to walk out, and I will never come back."

The level of resentment from the father and his threat to leave the family were disproportionate to what was being said.

"But this is important," said the therapist. "Would you,

Mr. Mitchell, I'm asking you to give your son your blessing as he leaves home to set out on his own.''

"What more blessing can you give than to give your moral support, your financial support. We've given it to him before.''

"You've given a great deal,'' said the therapist.

"And I'm very grateful,'' said Frank. "I don't want to give the impression that I'm not being grateful because it's not . . .''

"Then how can you sit there and say that you're not . . . ,'' interrupted the father.

"But I've just been raised on criticism,'' finished Frank.

The father made a gesture of irritation. As this conversation between Frank and the father was going on, Tommy was gesticulating and hissing with extreme tension.

"These are not working,'' said the father. "These sessions are not working.''

"Yes, they are,'' said Frank emphatically.

"I apologize, Mr. Mitchell,'' said the therapist, "because I must have conveyed to you a criticism and I didn't mean that. You've done a great deal for your son. I'm just asking you to say to him, 'Good luck, son, and I wish you well.' That's all I'm asking.''

"Happy birthday and good riddance,'' interjected Tommy.

"No, it's . . . don't you wish your brother good luck, too?''

"Yeah, I wish him good luck.''

"I don't think it's necessary to make him say that to me,'' said Frank, referring to the father.

" 'Cause he ain't gonna say it,'' said Tommy.

"You know he feels it,'' said the therapist.

"He probably feels it, but he just never or hardly ever verbalizes it,'' said Frank. "I'm sure that he—deep down inside there have been things that I've done that he's been proud of.'' As Frank talked, the mother sobbed loudly. "I'm sure of that. It's just that it's hardly ever been verbalized. Good job and, see, I need things like that. I think we all need that, don't we?''

"Have you heard the expression a two-way street?'' said the father.

It is possible that the cause for the resentment and alienation between the father and Frank was that the father, a working-class man with little education, felt a certain contempt for
the son's sensitivity, intellectual interests, and delicate tastes;
and Frank, in turn, felt contempt for the father's lack of sensitivity, intellectual interests, and education. This is a common
conflict when there is a difference in social class between father
and son. The father's comment about a two-way street spoke to
that effect.

"Can you give your dad some good words as you leave?"

"Sure," said Frank.

"You do that," said the therapist.

"He's provided a roof over my head, he paid for part of
my college expenses. But it requires more than working seven
days a week and providing material things. There's more to it,
isn't there?"

"Thank your father for what he's given you."

"I do thank you for all the material things you've given
me."

"Don't qualify. Just say thank you for your support."

"Thank you for your support."

"Many fathers kick out their sons at eighteen, you know."

"I'm trying to get across what I'm saying. There's just
been very little verbal encouragement throughout my life."

"I have, I've always said we're proud of you, Frank,"
said the father.

In a last effort to ease the separation, the supervisor suggested some words of wisdom to the therapist.

"You know," said the therapist, "in order to leave, a
young man has to leave with complaints, because there's so
much love that if there wasn't a complaint, he could not make
the break and could not leave. And so you know that there is
the appreciation but there has to be the complaint or he could
not break away and he could not leave. Mrs. Mitchell, will you
kiss your son?" The mother, crying, kissed Frank. "Mr. Mitchell,
I'd like you to shake his hand." The father shook Frank's hand
and immediately turned away. "Tommy, will you shake your
brother's hand?"

"Good luck, Frank. Hope, hope you . . . ," Tommy shook Frank's hand, unable to complete the sentence.

"Okay, Frank, will you be sure at least twice in this next week after you've moved out that you'll come back for dinner and that your mom will prepare a good dinner. Will you do that, Mrs. Mitchell?"

"Yes," said the mother, crying.

In a session that deals with separation, it is always important to ensure the continuity of the relationship.

"When do we have to come back?" asked the mother.

"Two weeks from today."

"I don't think I'll be able to come back," said the mother, crying.

A few days before the next session, Tommy called the institute and, referring to himself as Thomas, not Tommy, left the message that he could not come to the next session because he had found a construction job that was very important to him and he could not absent himself from it. The therapist called the parents, who said they were pleased with Thomas's job (from then on he was Thomas for everyone). The parents did not want to come to the session, so the therapist told them that therapy could be recessed, since it no longer seemed necessary. Thomas was not taking drugs, drinking, or behaving in delinquent ways, and he had a full-time job. These were the goals that the judge had set, and they had been achieved. The therapist suggested that, should any problem come up, the parents should call her. She would call them regularly to find out how things were going. Frank had moved out as planned and had come home for dinner.

Two months later, everything was still going well. The therapist asked the family to come for one brief interview so she could see Thomas and report to the court that he no longer needed therapy and his probation could be lifted. The parents were pleased. Thomas came to the interview looking completely different. He had changed from a tough motorcycle type with a bloated face into a polite, smiling, handsome young man. The following was a brief interchange during this session.

"You're really looking so good. You cut your hair and . . . do you have a girlfriend?" asked the therapist.

"Yeah," said Thomas.

"Ahh!"

Thomas touched his hair, "I just shampooed it."

"You look like you're fixed up for a girl. What's her name?"

"Rachel."

"Rachel. Have you been going with her for a while?"

"A couple of months now."

"So that's new in your life."

"Yeah."

"No wonder you're looking so good. You've got lots of things to look forward to."

After a few minutes of social conversation, the therapist thanked each one for coming and said to Thomas: "I assume you're not going to be the life ruiner any more."

"No," answered Thomas, smiling.

"I hope not," said the father.

Thomas had started dating his girlfriend a few days after the third session. He was very fond of her. She liked to go out to expensive places, so he became very interested in working and making money. He was laid off from the construction job but found another job soon after. A few months after this last interview, Frank became engaged and was soon married. The parents were pleased and gave him a trip to the Bahamas as a wedding present. About that time, Thomas moved out to an apartment with his girlfriend and got a job with the government, which did not pay very much but which offered him good educational opportunities. Ann lost her job and decided to go back to college, with the parents' encouragement. She was still living at home. The parents went away together on several trips and were enjoying each other.

To summarize, the therapeutic strategy in this case was based on the hypothesis that the conflict between Thomas and his father was a metaphor for the conflict between the father and Frank, and one conflict had replaced the other. Thomas's helpfulness in bringing the problem onto himself prevented his brother from resolving his differences with his father and therefore from feeling free to leave home. The goal of the therapy was to take the problem back to where it belonged so that it

could be discussed and resolved instead of being expressed
metaphorically through another conflict. Once Frank and his
father confronted each other explicitly, Thomas would be free
to get on with his life. To achieve this goal, the therapist used a
paradoxical intervention of prescribing the symptom with a
small modification of the context. It was suggested that the siblings take turns at being the "life ruiner," a term coined by
Thomas that described his position in the family. For two sessions, the therapist focused the conversation on a plan for first
Frank and then Ann to be the life ruiner. Even though the family opposed the idea, the discussion itself equalized the siblings,
and Thomas's behavior improved. By the third session, Frank
was explicit about his own contribution to life ruining in the
family, and his conflict with the father was out in the open.
Ann made an ineffectual attempt to call the problem upon herself but left the session without replacing her brother. After
these three sessions, Frank and Thomas were able to leave home
successfully, and each established a good relationship with a
woman outside the family. Ann decided to pursue a college career, and it is still to be seen if she will have difficulty leaving
home. Two years after the therapy, Thomas is still free of mental illness, alcoholism, drug abuse, and delinquency.

Sexual Problem of a Young Couple

The arguments of a couple about a certain issue may be a
metaphor for and replace their arguments about another issue
that is too painful or too threatening to the marriage to discuss
openly. Marital therapy can focus on both direct and indirect
methods for shifting from one level of argument to another and
for renegotiating the quid pro quo and establishing a better contract between the spouses.
    A young wife in her mid-twenties requested marital ther-
apy for a sexual problem. When the therapist called her to make
the first appointment, she explained that she and her husband
had been planning and saving their earnings during the four years
of their marriage for a trip. This trip was now only two months
away, but there was so much bad feeling between them because

of the sexual problem that they feared the trip would be ruined. In light of this information, it was apparent before the first interview that the therapy would have to be very brief so that the couple could go on their trip. Rather than ask them to postpone a trip they had planned since the beginning of the marriage, it would be better to solve the sexual problem as quickly as possible and let them go.

The supervisor planned that the therapist would conduct the first interview by asking husband and wife a series of questions covering several areas: the presenting problem, work, money, relations with relatives, how they had met, and what had attracted them to each other. Their answers to these questions would throw light on issues of power and hierarchy, the marital quid pro quo, and the metaphorical meaning of their interaction around the presenting problem.

The therapist began the first interview by asking the husband what the problem was. He answered: "She feels that we're not having enough sex, and it is my fault because she wants it and I don't."

"I just like to have, uh, sex more often than he does," said the wife. "We've been married for almost four years, and for a while it was very frequent, and now it's gotten down to . . ."

"Enough," said the husband.

"Once a week," said the wife, laughing, "and I always have to ask him."

"When I turn her down, that's upsetting by itself. When things are not working in that respect for whatever reason, she doesn't put up with it, or whatever. It's very upsetting."

"Who is it upsetting to?" asked the therapist.

"To me and to her."

The husband defined the problem as one in which he "turns her down." It may be that he was trying to present himself in a superior position as the one who had the power to put the wife down. If so, the question was, why?

"Let's see, you are a lab assistant, and you are a sales manager. Could you tell me a little bit about your job?" asked the therapist.

"I work in a private lab," said the wife. "I do radiology work, lab work."

"Do you like your work?"

"Yeah, I do. I enjoy it very much. I find it very rewarding."

"No, you don't," said the husband.

"I like what I do. I don't like where I work right now," said the wife, with a little laugh.

"We're both terribly bored working. We both want to retire and do nothing," said the husband.

"You're ready for retirement?" asked the therapist.

"And have sex for the rest of our lives. Yeah, we are, we really are," answered the husband.

"I'm not bored. I'd like to find a job with more career-type move-up opportunities," said the wife, gesturing up with her hands.

"What you don't like to be is a lab assistant," said the husband. "It seems like the more I look at it" (extending his arm and pointing his hand down at the wife), "a lab assistant is just a peon with a high degree of technology information and that's it, and every job she goes to, she gets the same thing."

"I don't like working at a lab. I like to . . ." interrupted the wife.

"It's just, you know, you go do this and this and if you want to leave today, goodbye, you're fired. There's lots of lab assistants around."

Again the husband put the wife down. In a situation in which the wife was talking to a female therapist and trying to present herself as a competent professional woman, the husband dismissed her statements, contradicting what she was saying and describing her as a "peon." Again the question was: Why does the husband humiliate the wife in front of the therapist? Was he so far down in relation to her that he had to retaliate in this way?

The therapist asked the husband about his job.

"I am currently selling rugs, basically. That's what it is," he said. "Buying and selling rugs. It's antique rugs. Kind of interesting. I hate it. I hate the entire working for making money. It's very frustrating. I bring a lot of frustrations home."

The wife was a laboratory assistant in radiology and the husband was a rug salesman. Her job had superior status and required a higher level of education than his job did. It could be that the husband was intent on putting down the wife because he resented her superior position. The wife also presented herself as more of an upper-class person than he was. This was indicated by her manner, her clothes, and her body movement. Although they both were attractive, she was more so. It could be that she was also of superior status in other areas.

"What is your home like?" asked the therapist. "What kind of home do you live in?"

"We have a private . . ." said the husband.

"A house," completed the wife.

"A beautiful house," said the husband.

"With a dog and no kids," qualified the wife.

"With a dog and no kids," repeated the husband, with a little laugh.

"Are kids in the plan?"

"Yes, she doesn't believe it because I'm putting it off, but yes, definitely."

"She doesn't believe it because what?" asked the therapist.

"He's holding it off," answered the wife. "But I'm agreeable to wait a while until we get some traveling out of our systems and get some stable job that you might like," she said looking at her husband.

The husband not only was withholding sex from the wife. He also was withholding children.

"How did you meet?"

"I bought a rug from him," said the wife, laughing.

"I fell in love the minute she walked in. That was it."

"What was it that attracted you to each other?"

They both laughed.

"I don't know what I ever saw in you."

"I didn't like him very much."

"You said it was instant love," said the therapist.

"He liked me a lot, but I didn't like him very much at first."

"I was a sex fiend at that time," said the husband. "I was

single, just goofing off, and in a totally different trip. She
walked in and I said, 'God—everybody stand away.' Drove me
crazy—absolutely nuts."

The wife laughed.

"What attracted you to your husband?"

"Well, I was at a point where I was just out of school. I
didn't know where I was going or what I was going to do with
myself, because I had lived with my parents almost throughout
the whole time I was going to school and everything, so I was
getting ready to make a break and I didn't know how or when
or how I was going to do it. So then he showed up and he just
helped me out."

At the beginning of the relationship, the husband had
been in a superior position as an older, independent man who
had helped the wife separate from her parents. Possibly, as time
passed and the wife matured, the husband had not been able to
stay in this superior position and the couple had had to find a
new balance. It is one of the paradoxes of marriage that it often
serves the purpose of helping one of the spouses leave home.
The irony is that, as soon as the marriage takes place and the
spouse has left the parents, the marriage has lost its purpose; it
no longer serves the end for which it was intended, because this
end has already been accomplished.

"Could you tell me a little bit about your families?"

"He is an only child."

"An only child," said the husband, making a face. "We're
both of Spanish origin. She's from Cuba, I'm from Venezuela.
Our families are very close to both of us. We love to see them
all the time. I have a Jewish mother, although she's Catholic."
The wife laughed. "Her parents are very sophisticated, and
they leave us alone and they don't interfere, and they're very
nice."

"You have to write them invitations to come over to the
house, because they never come to the house," added the wife.

"Yeah, her parents never visit us. I don't know why, but I
think they always felt that Monica should be left alone to do
whatever she wanted to."

"Well, they leave all their kids alone. My father . . ."

"Yeah, especially you."

"Well, you're an only child and you are . . ." said the therapist.

"I have a family of seven."

"Where are you in that?"

"I'm number two. And my father's a lawyer, and he has office hours at night, every other day. So they never have any time. On their nights off they go out. They have parties. They have invitations. One can never get hold of my parents. So they don't bother us. They don't really have time to bother us."

"I am uncomfortable with that," said the husband. "I am uncomfortable with both ends. My mother isn't really a problem unless you let her be and there's very little you have to do to stop it. And Monica agrees, I think."

"She's a nice lady. She's a sweet lady."

"Her parents are really nice, too."

The wife's parents were very sophisticated, and her father was an attorney. Although both spouses were of Spanish origin, her English was perfect and his was not. These were other areas in which the wife had a superior position.

"So you have both your parents and an aunt. Is there anyone else?"

"I have a kid from a previous marriage," said the husband.

"Is it a boy?"

"Yeah, he's a boy—ten years old. Uh, I see him, not enough," said the husband with a nervous laugh. "When I get a chance, once every two weeks it's working out to, for short periods of time. Like this afternoon he gets out of school at 3:45. I pick him up, we go play tennis, go to a movie, have dinner. I spend as much time as I can with him. But I don't have very much more time than that. Today's my day off, Sunday and Monday. But if he doesn't want to go out or come to the house on a Sunday or we don't feel like bringing him or—then I have to see him when I have some time."

"But he does come to the house on occasion?" asked the therapist.

"Occasionally. Occasionally. That's a source of problems between us. Monica doesn't feel totally comfortable with him."

The wife had been sitting listening to him with a finger covering her mouth.

"With?" asked the therapist.

"With Michael," said the wife.

"His name is Michael."

"Who does Michael live with?" asked the therapist.

"His mother," said the husband.

"How long were you married before?"

"Five years, four and a half years," said the husband, counting with his fingers, making faces, rubbing the back of his neck, and opening his shirt as if he were hot. The wife laughed. "Four and a half years and divorced for five I think."

"Did, by the way, did you sell her a rug that day she came in?" asked the therapist, laughing.

"I never sold her a rug," said the husband. "She had bought a rug from another salesman."

The issue of the husband's son was obviously an important one, for various reasons. The husband said that he did not see enough of his son, that the son did not visit the house often, and that his wife did not feel totally comfortable with him. It was the first time he had said that something was "a source of problems" between his wife and him. The wife sat very seriously, covering her mouth with her hand and conveying that there was something she did not want to say. The husband appeared hot and uncomfortable. These were all clear signs that this was an important issue, but there was one other sign that, for a supervisor, unmistakably defined an issue that must be addressed. That sign was that the therapist abruptly changed the subject and took the couple back to a happier time —their courtship days, when the wife had walked into the husband's store. The therapist had had a plan: to cover a series of areas in the couple's life by asking first one a question and then the other. After asking the husband about his son, she was supposed to turn to the wife and ask her about the child. The tension in the room must have been so great at that time that the therapist forgot her plan, changed the subject, and took the couple back to a happier period of their lives.

"Let me get that right about your family," said the therapist to the wife.

"There's six other children."

"Who of the six are you the closest to?"

"My little brother. He's nine. My sister and I lived together in Pittsburgh with a foster family. That goes back to when we were young. When I was eight years old, my parents sent us from Cuba. They sent three of their children ahead of them to the States, and they thought they were going to come right after us—come out of Cuba. They could not get visas or anything. That was when Castro, everything was coming apart, around '61. My sister and I lived with an American family in Pittsburgh for four years, and my brother lived with another family near Pittsburgh. So after four years my parents did finally get a visa and come through. They had all sorts of problems. Castro at first didn't let professionals come out of Cuba. And they had trouble getting visas. Then they stopped the freedom flights, and finally, after four years, they came through. And I guess that my sister is the closest to me. And then Mom had Andy, who's the little one, he's nine years old, in the States. And we all brought him up, you know, the rest of the family. I was like eighteen when he was born. So the rest of the family kind of brought him up."

"And he's the one you feel the closest to now?"

"Yeah. I always take him presents. I guess it's 'cause he's little."

When the wife was sent to a foster family in a foreign country at age eight and it took the family four years instead of one month, as she was told, to get together again, she may have thought that they had given her away. In those days, there was no communication with Cuba, no phone calls, no mail—and four years is a very long time for a child. The wife had had as much rejection in her life as a person could tolerate, and when her husband rejected her emotionally and sexually, he was hurting her in the way that hurt her the most.

Another consideration was that the wife's younger brother was almost the same age as the husband's son. It was possible that she related to her stepson more as an older sister than as a mother because of her experience in relating to a brother of that age.

The couple proceeded to talk about the relationship between the wife's parents, and their comments could be seen as metaphorical of their own relationship.

"Mom is very dependent on Dad. Dad, he always took care of Mother," said the wife.

"She resents this," added the husband.

"He patronizes her a lot. But they've always lived like that. They've gotten along like that."

"It's a Spanish set-up, you see. That's . . ."

"It's good for them. It works good for them," interrupted the wife.

"It might be bad, but that's the way we all have been brought up. In the Spanish family the father is the . . ."

"Is the boss. Mother consults with father," interjected the wife.

"Right. But she's got a lot of power, and it's still a matriarchal society."

"Not in my family," said the wife. "Dad's always the boss. And whenever there's a problem, Dad solves it!"

"It seems like that," said the husband. "In my house it may be the same thing, mostly because that's the way she sets it up lots of times, and I take advantage of it. I make the decisions. She refuses sometimes to take responsibility for something even if I say you have to do it. I keep telling her, 'Watch out, because one of these days you're going to want your freedom; then you're going to resent me for all the bad things I did to you. And then you're going to go out there and try to be a new woman. Then you're going to make a mess for me and I'm going to kick you right on the butt and say goodbye.' "

"But no, you see, I have the best of both worlds," said the wife.

"At this point, I'm really afraid of that. When she gets to be thirty-eight, which is a long time, it seems, from right now, she might say, 'Well, more power to me' and all this baloney and I wish she did it right now, right this second. She started getting more independent, gradually more independent, so it wouldn't be an explosion."

"See, at home I'm dependent," said the wife, "but when I'm working, when I'm with other people, I . . ."

"I certainly hope not," interrupted the husband, laughing. The wife also laughed and they winked at each other and gave each other little kicks. "That would be tragic."

"I'm a very aggressive, I'm a really assertive person," said the wife.

The wife had brought up her father's superiority, and the husband changed the conversation to a discussion of his own superiority over his wife and his fear that one day she would suddenly want too much independence and he would expel her. Once more the husband's gross attempts to proclaim a superior position over the wife led one to suspect that he was reacting against the wife's superiority and power. It could be that the wife was putting him down in ways that had become intolerable for him. However, it was a good prognostic sign for the relationship that, in a moment of tension, the couple had been able to overcome the bad feeling, laugh, and touch each other, and the unpleasantness had dissolved.

The therapist proceeded to ask about their sex life in the past and in the present.

"The first year of our marriage," answered the husband, "of getting to know each other, we never hopped out of bed. We were always in bed, or in the car. We would have sex right here if we could."

"I would come home for lunch," interrupted the wife.

"Lots of times we did it—in the store, anyplace. We just . . . it was constantly having sex."

"Insatiable," added the wife.

"Now when you do have sex, is it pleasurable?" asked the therapist.

"Not very," said the wife.

"Hm, hm," said the husband.

"What are your thoughts about that, Mr. Santos?"

"Yes, it's awkward sometimes, when there's pressure."

" 'Cause there's too many resentments," added the wife.

"Right, but it is pleasurable," said the husband.

"I think, on my part, I just think that he's not doing it because he wants to," said the wife. "I don't feel, I don't get what I want out of it, which is, you know, to feel like I'm wanted."

Next the therapist saw the husband alone for a few minutes to ask him about possible extramarital relationships. Although improbable, it could be that his lack of sexual interest in his wife was related to an involvement with another woman. After the wife had left the room, the therapist said, "Now, is there anything, Mr. Santos, that you would like to tell me privately now that she's gone?"

"I don't think there's anything that she doesn't know, I don't think. Only the aggravation and the anger that I feel on having to perform, on having to provide sex, on being a service for her, and I hate to put it in this way because it sounds awfully selfish and awfully personal. But I feel that way. And I remember my ex-wife being on the opposite end, because I wanted sex and she didn't. In our case it was extreme. We didn't have sex for two years."

"Is there any problem with other relationships outside the marriage?"

"With my kid. Because it's difficult. But that's all."

"You described that you were feeling pushed to have sex."

"To put out, you know, open your legs, spread 'em apart, and fuck. I hate it. I dislike it very much. At the same time, I know how bad she wants it."

This "macho" statement was not very believable. Again the question was: Why does the husband have to protest his superiority so much? The therapist was thinking of another woman as the cause of the problem, and the husband was thinking of his son. Once more the therapist changed the conversation abruptly when the child was mentioned.

"But is it enjoyable when you do have sex?" asked the therapist.

"Yeah, because I am very strong minded and she always is easily manageable. That is an advantage and a disadvantage. But I don't put out when I don't want to. And the times when it's really pressuring, even if I give in to it, it's bad. You know how it can be, terrible. I mean, she feels bad, I feel terrible, and it ends up being a nasty thing. I have to console her, she cries. It becomes very sensitive, very bad."

"I think that's pretty clear. Is there any other woman that you're seeing now? Are you having an affair?"

"I wish," said the husband, laughing.

"You wish?"

"Lots of them. No, I did a lot of that a while back. I really would like to have affairs, but somehow, when it gets right down to it, it's boring even to go after them. Maybe if somebody just came in and carried me to it I might do it. But I would feel guilty. I would feel bad." He sighed.

After this interview, during the week between the first and second sessions, the supervisor carefully considered all the information that had been obtained from the couple. On the basis of this information, she worked to develop a hypothesis about the presenting problem that would lead to a strategy for change. The questions the supervisor asked herself were: If the husband's sexual rejection of the wife was a metaphor, what other similar interaction did it replace? What was the marital quid pro quo? What was the balance, the tit-for-tat, involved in the husband's refusal to have sex? How did the presenting problem define each spouse's power and weakness in relation to the other spouse?

The wife appeared to be in a superior position to the husband in many areas: social status, education, work, and so on. In some areas, she did not hesitate to put down her husband, as in relation to her father. But in one area her superior position had become intolerable to the husband, and that was her rejection of his child. The couple seemed able to handle all other areas of hierarchical imbalance and to overcome them with a smile, a wink, or an affectionate gesture. The husband's rejection of the wife sexually was a metaphor for her rejection of his son, a problem about which the couple probably had argued for a long time. At some point, these arguments had become too stressful or had escalated too much for them to tolerate. The husband then began to refuse sex, and the couple began to argue about the husband's rejection of the wife in the same way they previously had argued about the wife's rejection of the child.

In terms of quid pro quo, the husband's rejection of the wife was a way of getting back at her for her rejection of his son. In terms of hierarchy, the husband's rejection of the wife placed him in a superior position in relation to her, but, at the same time, it defined his inferiority as a husband with sexual difficulties. The wife was in a superior position as the nonsymptomatic member of the couple, but she was in an inferior position as a rejected wife. The presenting problem was a source of power and helplessness for both spouses.

A simple way to resolve the problem was to establish a better quid pro quo in which the wife would be nice to the child and the husband would have sex more often with the wife. But the spouses were likely to reject this new contract if it were directly suggested by the therapist; it had to be arrived at spontaneously by the couple. The plan for the therapy was to request that the wife change her behavior toward the husband's son. The expectation was that, if the wife could be held long enough to a more kindly position, the husband gradually would become more affectionate and sexually interested in her. In this way they could reach a new quid pro quo.

The second session began with the therapist and husband discussing the husband's relationships with his wife and with his son.

"I was thinking about our talk last week, and we kind of passed over pretty quickly about your son. I recall that you said that he doesn't visit you in the home."

"He does. Once in a while. Not as often as . . . ," said the husband.

"Not as often as he could," completed the therapist.

"Not as often as he should," said the husband.

"I'm sure this is an area that must concern you and mean a lot to you. You are father and son, and you are not with him as much as you would like to be."

"True," said the husband.

"And that's a very important relationship. In fact, your son and your wife, I imagine, are the two most important relationships . . ."

"You're right," interjected the husband.

". . . that you have. And I was wondering what can be done to make that work better for you as his father."

"Well, it's difficult. Monica has always had a problem dealing with him. Not so much with him as with the fact that he's part of another family, of my other family. There's a certain resentment. It's difficult for her, and when he comes I see how difficult it is. Lots of times I just don't even want to bring it up."

It is possible to understand the husband's statement about his feelings with regard to the relationship between his wife and his son ("lots of times I just don't even want to bring it up") as a metaphor for his sexual feelings toward his wife.

"I try to do whatever I can to spend time with him. When Monica gets upset, I get upset, the kid naturally gets upset. I mean he knows that something is wrong. But (sigh), ahh, I understand to a certain extent. I think, I do think Monica should make a stronger effort. And I don't understand how anyone cannot just absorb a kid. Period. I don't care whose kid it is. It's just a kid in need of attention, caring, love, whatever adults must give. Especially if it is to someone that is part of your family."

"A very important part for you," said the therapist.

"And, on the other side, I cannot force Monica to do something that she is not capable of doing or doesn't want to do."

"You don't take him out with you?" said the therapist to the wife.

"I don't go with them when they go out. Very rarely."

"You don't share that kind of time with your husband?"

"I don't like to. See, when we were first dating and we first got married, we used to go out with him a lot together. Things were pretty good. Then there was a point where I just started resenting him. Carlos was kind of using him against me every once in a while and I don't remember exactly what it was but there was one episode where I just said, 'I've had enough of that kid, and I'm not going anywhere when Carlos and Michael go together.' "

"And you let her stay home?"

"Um, in other words I tend to avoid the problem," said the husband, with a sigh. "And it doesn't really bother me that much that she does not want to get involved in it. I would rather that she did and I would rather that we were a happy family and we went camping together and all that stuff, but if it doesn't happen I'm not about to make it a bigger problem."

"I have a plan," said the therapist. "You're in the best position to teach your wife about your son. Mrs. Santos, I'd like you to say to your husband that 'From now on I'm going to help you make a solid family relationship between the three of us and help you with your son,' and that you're willing to do that."

"I don't want to ask her that," said the husband.

"I'm asking her to say that to you."

"Ah!"

"Well, I didn't finish before. After I started resenting him . . . ," said the wife.

"We don't need to worry about before, because now it's a fresh start," interrupted the therapist. "It's a fresh start, and you're his wife and you love him. I can see that. You care a great deal for your husband. And part of that is the family that you actually do have. You actually do have Michael as part of the family because he's your husband's son."

"If you can make that change I could give you more credit than you've ever imagined," said the husband to his wife.

The husband's promise of "credit" may be a euphemism for a promise of sex.

"Yeah, but you're asking for it," said Monica.

"So, just say to him, turn to him and say to him that, 'Starting today I'm going to make every effort to help you and your son and to do what you want me to do for our family.' "

"I will make every effort to do what you want me to do, but you have to tell me first."

"It's up to you," said the husband, moved.

"Um hmm. And shake hands."

The husband repeated, with an anxious laugh, "It's up to you," and the spouses shook hands.

With regard to this intervention, it is appropriate to make a comparison between the strategic approach and other schools of family therapy. Probably any family therapist would have understood that this couple's sexual problem was related to the couple's conflict about the husband's son. However, the difference between the strategic approach and other schools lies in what the therapist does to solve the problem. Other therapists might have had the spouses express their wishes and feelings and embark on negotiations about the child; in a conflict that had developed over more than four years, old resentments would have been brought up and negotiations might have been long and difficult. In this strategic therapy, the therapist avoided these discussions and simply told the couple what to do. She did not want to hear about the wife's feelings or the story of her past resentments. When the husband protected the wife from changing by saying "I don't want to ask her that," the therapist took responsibility for the change she was requesting and said, "I'm asking her." It is clear that the sequence of interaction between husband and wife involved not only the wife's rejection of the son and the husband's sexual rejection of the wife but also the husband's support of the wife's rejection of the child and his interference with any attempts by her to change. This behavior is typical of a biological parent who wishes to involve the stepparent but at the same time is reluctant to allow this involvement. The therapist's straightforward directive to the wife to promise to help the husband with his son is based on two assumptions. One is that a therapist can and should take responsibility for bringing people together in positive ways. The other is that, although people do feel or think what they say, they do not necessarily think or feel first and then express themselves. If the wife says that she is willing "to make every effort" to help her husband, it is likely that she will feel that way. In contrast, had she been asked whether she was willing to make every effort, she probably would have said, "No."

The therapist said, "And you, Mr. Santos, can tell your wife that you're going to make sure that you will let her know exactly what to do to help you with your son."

"I'll tell you what to do. It's not a big deal," said the husband. He had begun to cry quietly.

"I didn't hear that," said the therapist.

"I said I'll tell you what to do and help you out with him. It's not a big deal, it's pretty easy." The husband sniffled, trying to hold back his tears.

"You want to shake on that?" asked the therapist.

The husband said, "Yeah," and they shook hands.

"Now we need to make a plan for this week, and I think this is where we really need to work. Let's plan a time. This is real important for you, isn't it Mr. Santos?"

The husband was drying his tears with his hands. He sighed and said, "Yeah." He picked up a tissue and dried his eyes. "I have a lot of guilty feelings about the whole thing from way before she showed up. So, yeah, it's difficult. I'm not sure I will be tremendously happy when my kid is spending every day at my house, either," he laughed, "to be totally honest with you."

The husband's tears confirmed the importance of the issue with his son. But even when he was crying, he attempted to minimize the wife's guilt and protect her by taking responsibility himself and expressing ambivalence toward the child.

"Well, look who's gonna have it worse," said the wife.

"I know, I know."

"But you've got a commitment from Mrs. Santos to help you with this as long as you can teach her what to do, and you're going to teach her what to do. You're more experienced about your son's meaning to you. That bond between you and your son, you know best about. She hasn't had much experience in what it means to have a son and to be a father to a son, especially."

"I guess not," said the husband.

"But the conflict isn't that we don't know what to do, that I don't know what to do with him. It's that it takes him away to another person and I don't like him to . . ."

"It's not so much losing him if he gives more to his son, but you're going to get more of your husband," said the therapist. "Now, maybe you ought to give your husband a hug and a kiss, because he's obviously having a lot of feelings about this."

The husband sighed and the wife stood up, went over to her husband, and gave him a long hug.

"I don't need all this," said the husband, laughing. "I don't need all this."

"You're a very loving man and you're showing it, and it's important that she recognize this. I think she's been getting away with a lot."

The husband laughed.

"I know," said the wife with a little smile.

"Let's make a plan," said the therapist. "Now what is a good day that he can come and visit you?"

"I guess on Sunday," said the husband. "Saturday night through Sunday."

"Okay, how would you like that visit to be? Specific things that she could do for your son while he's there."

"I would say choose a time, ten minutes or a half an hour, as much as you can stand, or want to, to really interact with him, and not to be correcting him or parent-like, saying 'Well, Michael, this is not the way this is done,' or something like that. But just talk to him, and poke him, and give him a hug, and kick him in the butt. He's a big kid, you know. All I need is the kid to realize that . . . he's not going to think that you love him to death or anything like that, but he's going to see that you're trying to be nice to him, and that's all that is needed all through the weekend."

"Yes," said the wife in a little voice, as she began to cry and reached out for the tissues. Crying softly and holding a tissue to her eyes, she said, "I don't want to do it."

The wife's tears seemed such an extreme response to what the husband was saying that the supervisor behind the mirror began to think that perhaps there was something intolerable about the child. She called the therapist and asked her to inquire about the boy's behavior.

"I'm wondering what it is that's so difficult, what it is that he does," said the therapist.

"That Michael does?" asked the wife.

"Yes, how does he behave?"

"He can be obnoxious sometimes," said the husband.

"But he's not obnoxious to me," said the wife. "If I'm nice to him, he's nice back."

"If you're not nice to him, he's still nice back," said the husband.

"Most of the time," she said. "He ignores me if I say something not nice. It's just a big problem. I've made it be real big."

"Yeah. It's not a big problem. It's a little problem that you made big. That's for sure," said the husband.

"Yes," said the wife.

"I really don't know what triggered it," said the husband.

"Is it the way he behaves?"

"It was because a long time ago . . . ," said the wife.

"No, he's super good," said the husband.

"No, he's a brat sometimes," corrected the wife, "a real behavior-problem kid."

"What does he do?"

"He doesn't do anything when he's with his dad and me, because he gets all the attention he wants and he's pretty happy. But he can be a nasty kid."

"With you—he can be nasty?"

"No, I know I'm contradicting myself. No, he's not nasty with me."

Later in the interview, the husband instructed his wife: "You don't have to be kissing him, hugging him, and feeding him. You just do what you always do . . . except, it's going to be difficult because it's a prescription. You're going to have to remember to do that. And you cannot resent it, because if you resent it like hell what good is it?"

"No, I won't resent it."

"And do it regularly. And the next morning when we feed him breakfast, if he looks anxious to eat because he's always hungry, don't make fun of him."

"Okay."

The first step in the therapy plan had been accomplished, and the wife had promised to change. It was now necessary to find ways of holding her to this change for a few weeks until the husband's behavior toward her began to change, since changes in interaction require some time to develop and stabilize. The problem in therapy is often how to hold a family member to a change for a number of weeks until the other family members can change in turn. The therapist suggested to the husband: "I think that if you can do something really special with her Thursday and Friday nights, that will get her in the mood for Saturday."

"A little positive reinforcement," laughed the wife.

"Fine, fine," said the husband.

"The closer you get to Michael, the more you're going to have him, the more you can do for Michael and the more he's going to need you and need to be with you as a result."

"But, you see, I got him anyway," whined the wife in a childish voice. "That's why I never had to do anything."

"You've got part of him. The other part includes Michael. You want all of him, and that goes with it. That's always going to be," said the therapist, speaking metaphorically, "because Michael is his son."

The session ended with a paradoxical suggestion that the wife would give the husband a hard time that week. It was clear that the wife had accepted as much direction from the therapist as she could tolerate. She would certainly refuse to follow whatever new suggestion was given. Therefore, it was suggested that she give her husband a hard time as a way of ensuring that that would not happen.

"Now I have a feeling she's going to give you a hard time this week." The wife laughed. "But I can tell just from watching how you've handled this discussion today, I can see you're a strong man and you have strong feelings about your son and you're really getting things in charge here today. And you clearly want to go through with this, and I think she is going to give you a bit of a hard time this week. But I know you can handle it and it will go well."

"No, I won't give you a hard time," said the wife.

"I know you won't. I tell you if she says to me, 'I won't give you a hard time,' she won't. Just because if she decides she is going to do it she'll do it so well that it'll seem like why in the hell didn't she do it before. And she'll even enjoy herself. And it's not like she had to go and take a pill every ten minutes to be able to do it. She'll have a good time, she'll enjoy it, she'll come up with surprises."

"Then why did you let me get away with not doing it?" said the wife.

"Because it's your problem. It's your damn decision. I can't make those decisions for you. They're too deep, they're too important for me to hit you over the head and make you do it."

That was the end of the second session. The third session began with the wife saying: "I did all my good deeds."

She had been very nice to Michael that weekend. Change had begun, but a way still needed to be found to hold the wife to a kindly position until a new quid pro quo could be established. The husband related how she had complained to him. "She feels that we came here so I would make more love to her," he laughed nervously, "and I ended up playing with my kid. You know, she's right."

"Logically it doesn't look like one is going to lead into the other," said the wife, tearfully.

The husband defended the therapist's approach: "You know I've resented you for that for a long time. You know, I never understood why in the hell you can't deal with a kid."

"So then you take away the thing that I like the most, right?"

"The hell if I did it on purpose. Just like you don't make Michael's problem on purpose. You know, maybe that's the way it works, and it's nature's built-in way of saying, 'you screw me, I'll screw you—or not.' " They both laughed.

The rest of the session was devoted to planning what the couple would do in the next two weeks with the son and what nice things the husband would do for the wife.

The fourth session began with a report on the activities of the past two weeks. The couple had done everything that was planned and had enjoyed Michael. The therapist asked: "How many times a week are you now having sex?"

"A couple, three at best, and that doesn't happen that often," said the husband.

"Yes, I agree."

"And that isn't what you were hoping?" asked the therapist.

"Well, yes, it is, but it's not that spontaneous," said the wife.

"I think I'd rather have more sex also. There is a certain amount of strain there that prevents me from doing it."

"Are you able to have orgasms?" the therapist asked the wife.

"No, generally, well, sometimes, but not as satisfying."

"And that's something you'd like to change?"

The wife answered tearfully: "Yes, I think the reason that . . . What I like most about making love with Carlos is to have him do it, to have him make me feel good, to make me feel like a woman, to have him do it. And when I have to do it for myself, it's not good. But I can do it to myself. I can make myself come to orgasm, but it's not him."

"You have a faculty that millions of women are looking for, and you complain about it, for God's sake," laughed the husband.

"Well, she seems to question whether you are sincere. She's a lovely woman, and she's a turned-on woman, which are things that you obviously really appreciate in her. I'm not sure that you believe that he feels that way about you. I can tell from your crying." The wife laughed through her tears. "Mr. Santos, turn to her and really let her know that she turns you on."

The husband turned toward the wife: "I haven't stopped. I think you know that. You should by now. I haven't stopped caring for you, loving you, and being turned on by you."

This is an example of asking someone to express what the therapist wants him to feel and not necessarily what he would express if asked to explain his feelings. The therapist asked the husband to tell the wife that she turns him on. Had the therapist instead asked the husband whether he was interested in his wife, it is possible that he would have answered, "Not as much as before," "I'm too used to her," "There are too many resentments," or the like. The wife then would have felt more rejected, and it would have become more difficult for the therapist to improve the relationship. In asking the husband to tell his wife that she turns him on, the therapist assumed that he would feel what he said and therefore that, after saying it, he would be more convinced that she does turn him on.

Later in the interview, the wife said, "Before we came here I thought that he didn't enjoy sex and he didn't do it for me. But since we've been coming here I feel like, like you pointed out to me, that he resents me," she sobbed, "and I feel like it's gotten worse because of that."

During the previous two weeks, the wife had been nagging the husband constantly about their sexual life and waking him up at two o'clock in the morning to discuss their relationship. Although she was still behaving kindly toward Michael, the husband's behavior toward her had not yet changed sufficiently. The therapist used a paradoxical intervention to block the couple's negative interaction so that positive changes could take place.

"I'd like you to take a few minutes each way, maybe four minutes each one of you, and I want you, first, Mrs. Santos, just to express all your worries to Mr. Santos about . . . 'You don't really mean it. You really don't want to make love to me. You resent me. You don't like what I'm doing with Michael. I don't think you really want to have sex. You didn't start it.' I want you to really tell him everything you're worried about."

"To nag him," said the wife.

"Oh, this is going to be the best time you ever had," interjected the husband.

"You've got four minutes to do that, and I want you to take all four minutes," said the therapist. Then she turned to the husband: "You'll get your turn after this."

"Well, he already knows it," laughed the wife, still tearful.

"Oh, come on, you can do better than that," said the husband. "Imagine it's two in the morning and you can't go to sleep."

"Mr. Santos, she's going to do this. She's going to do this."

"About him," said the wife, pointing to her husband. "Right?"

"Yes, all these things that you're concerned about. All these worries you have."

"I'm worried about that . . . when we make love it's not good."

"It's not good, you don't love me," said the therapist, imitating the wife's childish manner and making her laugh. "You don't want to have sex with me. Come on, just like that."

"It's not good and you don't want to do it, it's like somebody made you," said the wife.

"I have to force you to make love to me. Now say it," coached the therapist.

"I have to force you to make love to me. I wish you would just get up and attack me all by yourself," said the wife tearfully. "If I didn't start it, you'd just roll over and go to sleep. And you'd let that nice erection go to waste," she giggled mischievously.

The husband gestured for her to continue: "Michael, Michael."

"And this weekend, when we weren't going to do anything, what did you do? You went out with Michael and left me there after making a big deal about staying home. And then you took him out and I had to answer the phone, and that wasn't very fair."

"Mr. Santos, now you have three or four minutes," said the therapist.

"I really think that what happens," said the husband, "you have to have a problem. I even think when you talk about how it used to be, how good it used to be before, uh, you forget that we had problems back then. You're almost talking like you were back in Cuba—how nice it was back then. You don't even remember what it was like back then. All you do is complain about my sexual performance. All you do is complain about when I do have sex with you."

"But when I didn't complain about it, it didn't help," interrupted the wife.

The husband raised his voice: "Shut up. You just listen. When we have sex you still don't like it. At least you say you don't like it, and that really bothers me. Because I see you enjoying the heck out of it. I see you having orgasms."

"Oh, Carlos, that's not fair."

"Okay," said the therapist. "You've had your three min-

utes. That's very good and you did well, too. I think you could
be a little more . . ."

"Flourishes—ruffles and flourishes," said the wife.

"Yes, and you took about four minutes each way. And
over the next two weeks what I want you to do is, every day I
want you to sit down in . . . do you have a dining room table?"

"Yes."

"Okay. I want you to sit down at the dining room table
and spend seven minutes each way talking like this."

"Can I answer back?" asked the wife.

"You spend seven minutes and you can complain and nag
or express yourself like you were doing right here, and then he
gets his seven minutes and he can do just what he did here back
to you. I want you to do this every day for two weeks and I
want you to keep some notes about it and bring like a diary of
how it went. Now at no other time during the day or night can
you complain or discuss this. Just during the seven minutes."

"And he gets the floor and I don't answer back?" asked
the wife.

"That's right," said the husband.

"Well, when you get the floor he doesn't answer back,"
said the therapist.

"Well then, what if we come up with a problem? Do we
talk about it later?" asked the wife.

"No," answered the therapist.

"No," said the husband.

"It's all in that seven minutes," said the therapist.

"I love this," said the husband.

"You just hear the problems?" asked the wife.

"All I have to do is seven minutes," said the husband.

"Don't you have to solve it?" asked the wife.

"No. You just bullshit about it," said the husband.

"Well, then you'll go on feeling bad the whole rest of the
night," said the wife, while the husband laughed. "Well, what if
we hate each other . . ."

"Well, you get your seven minutes every day. It's guaranteed," said the therapist.

"Who's first?" said the wife, and the husband laughed.

"Okay, that's a very good question. Who's going to be first?" said the therapist.

"You're last," said the husband.

"Every other day we'll take turns," said the wife emphatically.

With this directive, under the guise of improving communication about problems, communication was in fact blocked. Each spouse could complain but could not answer the other's complaints. The paradoxical directive prescribed the same complaining behavior the wife was presenting, but with a small modification of the context. The where, the when, and the how were changed. The directive to complain was also given to the husband, because it was assumed that he must be covertly critical of the wife if she continued to nag him so much. If complaints were explicit and arguments blocked, it would be possible for the spouses to change to satisfy each other's needs.

In the fifth session two weeks later, the couple reported laughingly that they had been unable to fill seven minutes with complaints every day, and so they had reread their notes on each other's complaints.

"We were having a good time," said the wife.

"You weren't supposed to have a good time doing it."

"Well, I would look forward to doing it so that I could get all these things out of my system," said the wife.

"Sometimes we got angry," said the husband.

"One time he got real mad because I made faces," laughed the wife.

"She was having fun. We knew what it was for, we weren't sitting there goofing off."

"I don't see what would be fun about doing it, because this wasn't part of the idea," said the therapist.

"Well, it was fun because the whole day you couldn't complain or anything," said the wife, "and when it finally came time to say what you felt, it was enjoyable to let the other person know what was wrong. I wrote what he said and he wrote what I said."

"Well, how did things go in general during the last two weeks?"

"It was pretty good," said the wife.

"We've had a pretty pacific week," said the husband. "We didn't have any fights. The seven minutes took up the fact that, it was like we couldn't fight, so little things never came up."

"Did you see Michael over the weekends?"

"Yeah, we've seen him a lot. We've been seeing him an awful lot."

"Both weekends," said the wife.

"And how was that? How did that go?"

"It was very enjoyable. I mean I thought I did pretty good."

"Did she do pretty good?"

"Yes. Yes," said the husband.

The couple talked about how they had gone camping with Michael, which, at the beginning of the therapy, the husband had mentioned that he wanted to do.

"So you had a pretty good two weeks," said the therapist.

"Well, see, Monica, from the time that we made our deal, has been trying very hard, and I know, I can tell, that sometimes it's been difficult. I don't say it's not."

"Well, see, it wasn't a deal, Carlos. I always had it in me, but you never asked me to do it."

"So how has your love life been for the last two weeks?"

"Pretty good," said the wife.

"It's better than before, I think . . . somewhat," said the husband.

"I don't think it's better. It's just still good," said the wife, as if she had never complained about it.

"Oh, well, that's an improvement. It used to be lousy," said the husband, and the wife laughed.

The same paradoxical directive was given for the next two weeks, with the addition that the wife was to "pretend" to complain about sex rather than actually complain. In that way, if the wife complained about sex, the husband would not know if she was really complaining or just following the directive to pretend, and he would not respond in his usual ways.

In the sixth session, the couple reported that during the

last week they had not used the seven minutes of complaining very much.

"I think we used it when we needed it, and we didn't need it that much. We had a couple of quick outbursts or fights, but it's like it's not really a fight. And we had one situation that was a little difficult, at least," said the husband.

"So I made him sit down at the bargaining table so we could argue about it," said the wife.

"It's a real nice tool," added the husband. "It's a release at a certain point because, you know, 'I'll kill you!' 'You have seven minutes.' " He laughed.

"So you find it's really useful when you need it," said the therapist.

"Well, we've made it useful," corrected the wife.

This was the last session before the couple went away on their trip, and the therapist said: "It's just been a real pleasure working with you. You're a fun couple, and you have an awful lot going for you."

"Thanks," said the husband. "I tell you we enjoyed this. I think it's worked in the short period of time that we had. I think it's worked a lot. It's helped a lot. I don't know how, but it has."

Then the wife presented a complaint that would finally lead to the formulation of a new marital contract. She said: "I have a complaint."

"A complaint about what?" asked the husband.

"About Carlos. He doesn't want anything to get in the way of his terrific weekends that he has planned for Michael, so he starts fights on purpose with me whenever I do a little thing to interfere with this terrific thing that he's doing. He takes offense very, very easily whenever I say something, disagree with something. If you'd give me more of a chance, if you weren't so negative. The minute I walk in the room, you're waiting for me to make a mistake. And if you'd let me know that you had more of an open mind, it certainly would help me."

"Look, it's not that I'm waiting for you to make a mistake. It's that I'm so afraid that you're gonna be pissed about something."

"Yes, see, you don't give me a break."

"I'm just afraid that you're gonna react in some kind of weird way."

"Well, why? Am I an ogre?"

"You can be, yes."

"I'll tell you what we can do. Here—let's take this paper and a pen and write down an agreement on how this is going to be solved. You can solve this right now and get it written down," said the therapist.

The couple were ready to arrive at a new quid pro quo.

"Okay, when I walk in the room, write this down," said the wife to her husband.

"Okay."

She laughed, "You won't think I'm going to be nasty, you'll think I'm going to be nice. And all week long you'll imagine thoughts of me being nice to Michael. And stop making me an ogre. And you give me half a chance." She paused and laughed again, "Can I have an addendum?"

"Yes. Addendum. P.S. P.S."

The wife laughed, "I can get all the sex I want if I'm nice to Michael."

They both laughed loudly.

"I knew it was coming, I could see the kitchen sink flying. . . . Eeaah," said the husband, bouncing the pen in the air.

"No, okay. I mean it."

"All the sex you can eat."

"If I'm nice."

"I'm gonna write it down. All the sex you can eat. Right?"

"If I'm nice to Michael."

"All the sex you can eat."

"You're going to have a good trip," said the therapist, and the couple laughed.

They went away on their trip and sent the therapist a postcard, saying, "We are enjoying our trip and each other." On follow-up ten months later, they were happy together and the wife was pregnant.

To summarize the therapy, issues of power, metaphors, and the marital quid pro quo were explored in the first interview. A plan for the therapy was based on the idea that the husband's rejection of his wife was a metaphor for her rejection of his son and was also a way of paying her back; one issue had replaced the other as a subject of controversy in the marriage. The problem was solved by helping the couple arrive at a new contract in which the husband would have sex more often with the wife if she was nice to his son. The therapist assumed that if the wife could be held for a time to positive behavior toward the child, the husband would respond positively toward her and the couple would spontaneously arrive at a new contract. The plan was carried out with some difficulty as the wife reluctantly changed, the husband slowly responded to her changes, and the couple became involved in lengthy discussions about their relationship. The therapist intentionally blocked these conversations with a paradoxical directive in which the when, the where, and the how of the couple's interaction were changed. By the sixth session, the couple's sexual problem had been solved, and they spontaneously wrote a contract making explicit the new quid pro quo.

3

Influencing Adults Through Children

When a parent presents a problem behavior, the unit for therapy is always in question: Will it be the parent as an individual, the parent and the spouse as a couple, or both parents and the children as a family? Typically, the parent is seen alone in individual therapy or with the spouse in marital therapy, depending on the therapist's orientation, the nature of the problem, and the availability of the spouse. Sometimes the parent is seen with his own parents, but rarely are his children included in the therapy. The parent might have a variety of problems, such as depression, anxiety, psychosomatic symptoms, drug addiction, or alcoholism, or he may be an incompetent parent, rejecting of the children, abusive, or neglectful. Whatever the problem, the therapist needs to determine what significant interaction in the parent's life will be taken into account in the therapy, what relationship will be the unit of intervention. The choices are usually limited to interactions with grandparents, spouse, children, or occasionally siblings or other relatives. Characteristically, a strategic therapist will see a parent alone or with the spouse but not with the grandparents or the children for fear of creating hierarchical problems or of burdening the children with difficulties that belong to an adult world.

Typically, the therapist will try to discover the origin of

the problem in terms of a conflict with a spouse or with the grandparents. The children are usually thought of as victims suffering the consequences of having a disturbed parent or as agents of provocation exacerbating the parent's problem; rarely are they considered as having the potential to initiate change. Rather, the therapist most often focuses on the adult members of the family in understanding the conflict related to the presenting problem and in designing a strategy to resolve it. In other words, the therapist generally relies on the adult members of the family to bring about change.

The Child as Change Agent

A different view is offered here. Instead of thinking about who are the parties involved in originating the problem, the therapist thinks about who are the parties that could be involved in resolving the problem. Children, whether very young, adolescents, or young adults, can be invaluable in this respect. As has been described elsewhere, symptomatic children can be devoted helpers of the family (Madanes, 1980, 1981b); the same is true for nonsymptomatic children.

Just as a parent may temporarily set aside his own problems to help a disturbed child, so may a parent respond positively to a child's attempts to change him. When an adult presents an involuntary symptom, marital problems, or abusive or delinquent behavior, relatives, friends, and professionals may try unsuccessfully to help. But when a child is the helper, the therapist can appeal to the special bond between parent and child. When the parent sees himself as protected by a child who loves him, he may focus his concern on the child who will help him overcome his own personal, economic, or social difficulties.

Children are always concerned about their parents, but they may express this concern in a variety of ways. They may just brood or worry about a parent, or they may misbehave or develop symptomatic behavior in an attempt to help the parent (Madanes, 1980; 1981b), but seldom does our culture provide them with the means to effectively help the parent. In Western society, children, until they become mature adults (and sometimes until they are middle-aged), are at the bottom of the hierarchy; they are to be cared for and protected by the parents, and not the other way around.

Hierarchical Reversal

A therapist, however, can reverse this situation. The therapist can actually put children in charge of some important aspect of the parents' lives. The children are then raised in the hierarchy in terms of power and responsibility, and they can effect change in a variety of ways. They can, with the support of the therapist: organize the household and their own behavior in relation to each other and to the parents; advise the parents on how they should behave and how they should conduct their own lives; offer the parents the love and caring that the parents may have previously rejected or been unable to elicit; influence the parents in metaphorical ways so that, for example, a parent will be led to imitate the competent and caring behavior of a child or so that the relationship between mother and father may be influenced to resemble the benevolent interaction between the children; or provoke the parents to respond to the contrast between their own incompetent and irresponsible behavior and the child's responsibility and caring by taking charge of their family and correcting the situation so that the children need no longer be in charge.

The fact that children can be used to correct a parent's problem does not imply that they are or are not causal to this problem. In this approach, the origin or cause of the problem is not a consideration. The therapist thinks only in terms of who can participate in resolving the problem. This approach is particularly useful when a parent presents a chronic problem that may have originated far in the past for reasons that are difficult if not impossible to determine, but the problem persists in the present because of a context and a sequence of interaction that sustains it.

A parent who has an addiction or who is delinquent, abusive, or neglectful of his children is condemned by society and loses authority and the respect of his family. Agents of social control (social workers, psychiatrists, psychologists, and others) investigate and supervise the parent, while at the same time trying to restore his confidence and competence. It is not necessary for a parent to be delinquent to lose control of his family: The intervention of psychiatrists and social workers in the life of a family can have the same effect of divesting the parent of authority and affect with respect to the children. In these cases, the therapist is presented with one or two characteristic hierarchical organizations. When one parent is delinquent and the other is not, usually the nonsymptomatic or nondelinquent parent is in control and excludes the other parent through a coalition with social agents and/or with the children against the parent with the problem. When the family has only one parent or when both parents are delinquent or symptomatic, either a parental child partially takes over the parents' responsibilities or no one takes them over and the family becomes disorganized. Sometimes the grandparents take over the family and exclude the parents.

From the point of view of strategic therapy, the problem is how to help the parent without putting him down. This is often difficult to accomplish, and indirect interventions may be particularly useful. Instead of attempting to raise the parent in the hierarchy, the therapist may put him down even more by giving authority to the children. When this is done skillfully, in a playful, caring way without insult, the results may be surprisingly positive for all concerned. The examples that follow illustrate this approach.*

The Father with a Pain in His Marriage

It would be impractical to put children in charge of the important aspects of their parents' lives, such as the parents' work, their sex lives, issues dealing with money, or their social relations. When a therapist wants to use the strategy of putting children in charge, he must find a way of doing so that will be

*The therapists in these cases were Penny Purcell, M.A., and Richard Spector, M.S.W.

feasible and that will not have unpredictable consequences. One such way is to arrange for the children to be in charge of the parents' happiness. The parents can be told that the children are in charge, but only in one area, and not a very important one—just happiness. The parents are to continue to take care of their affairs as usual, but their happiness will be governed by their children. When presented this way, parents readily agree, since happiness does not seem very important and they are willing to follow their children's directives.

A man in his early fifties was referred for court-ordered therapy. He was addicted to pain killers and, over a period of eleven years, had forged numerous prescriptions to obtain drugs. He had worked for twenty years as a printer, and during the last nine of those years he had forged prescription forms, to which he had easy access because of his job. He was not fired because his work was appreciated, but he had appeared in court numerous times, had suffered various penalties, and had a trial pending and the possibility of a jail sentence. His attempts to overcome his addiction had failed, and so had previous therapy. The man was married and had four children, three sons and one daughter. The second son was away at a seminary, studying to become a priest. The three other children, ranging in age from fourteen to twenty-two, were living at home.

Therapist and supervisor decided to see only the man and his wife in the first interview and to approach the problem as a marital one; the idea was to solve whatever marital problems were related to the addiction and delinquency and to arrange for the wife to help the husband in changing his behavior. When the couple came to the first interview, the husband immediately presented himself as an addict and took the blame for all the family's problems. The wife said that for ten years she had done everything she could, that she was tired of her husband's promises, had too many resentments, and was unwilling to do more. Both spouses appeared indifferent to the therapist, and it was clear that they were complying with the court order for compulsory therapy but did not think anything would come of it; they had been through this before.

In an attempt to define the problem as an interactional

one, the therapist suggested that the husband was addicted to
pain killers because he had pain and that someone in the family must be giving him the pain. The couple denied this, saying
that only *he* was to blame; but finally the husband said that the
children irritated him with their untidiness. The wife immediately jumped on the husband, defending the children with such
intensity and anger that it was clear that she was in a powerful
coalition with the children against him. As husband and wife
talked about their lives, it became evident that the wife also derived power from holding a superior position in practically all
areas. She had had more education than the husband, held a job
that was artistic and intellectual, was a competent housewife
and mother, led a rich spiritual life (she went to Mass every day),
and felt that she was a superior person in every way. She constantly put down the husband, but the husband never criticized
her. She accused the husband not only of being a bad husband
but also a bad father, irritable, insensitive, demanding, and cruel
to the children.

The therapist attempted to bring the couple together in
various ways, emphasizing their successes and their love for each
other, and suggested that the husband invite the wife to do
something with him outside the house; this was to be something
he would like to do, even though it might not be the wife's
favorite activity. The husband had great trouble deciding what
to ask the wife to do with him, but he finally came up with
going to a restaurant where he would like to have dinner and a
show that he would like to see.

At the second session, the couple reported that things between them were better. The oldest son had provoked the father, and the father had refused to quarrel with him; as a result,
the young man had apologized. The father related that this son
used drugs and that neither of the boys did any chores. The
therapist attempted to bring the couple together in agreement
as parents, but the father pointed out that it was difficult for
him to enforce anything, since he himself was an addict. The
mother blamed the father for all difficulties and reasserted her
coalition with the children against him.

It was clear that, although there had been improvement

since the first session, the therapy would be slow and painful if it continued to focus on direct attempts to bring the couple together as spouses and as parents. The wife's coalition with the children against the husband would prevail over the therapist's attempts to bring the spouses together. An indirect strategy of approaching the parents through their children might succeed in a shorter time and with less pain for all involved. The therapist asked the couple to bring the children to the next interview.

The two younger children (the couple's fourteen-year-old daughter and seventeen-year-old son) came to the next appointment, and the therapist took them into the therapy room, leaving the parents in the waiting room. She told the children that the father took medication because he had a pain in his marriage. She said that she had tried to help the parents be happy together but had failed because they had forgotten how to be happy and that she therefore needed the children's help. They would be in charge of the parents' happiness, and from then on it would be their responsibility to see that their parents had a happy marriage. Did the children agree to assume this responsibility, she asked, and would they help their parents so that they would be happy? The children timidly said yes. Both children appeared shy and worried, and the daughter seemed particularly depressed. They had obviously come to the session with some trepidation.

The therapist took paper and pencil, gave them to the boy, and asked the children to start making a list of the things they could arrange in the next two weeks so that the parents would experience happiness. For example, would it be possible to arrange a special dinner for the parents in the home, for which the children would set the table, cook, and serve, and which the parents could enjoy without having to prepare anything or wash the dishes afterwards? The children said that that would be possible, and the therapist began to discuss with them how the table should be set to create a special atmosphere that would make the parents happy and that would bring them together. They were to use the good tableware and tablecloth and cloth napkins instead of paper, and they were to provide candlelight to create a more romantic ambiance. The children agreed to all this and wrote it down. Then they discussed with the therapist what they could cook. It turned out that they only knew how to make hamburgers, so hamburgers and salad would be the menu. Children and therapist chose the day and time for the meal and decided how to give instructions to the older brother so that he would cooperate with the preparations. The children would serve the parents, and then they would eat in the kitchen after the parents were finished. As this conversation progressed, the children became more vivacious, and the son wrote down their decisions with enthusiasm.

The son suggested that the parents should go out one evening to dinner and a movie. There was some discussion about which movie they should see, and the children agreed on one that both parents might like. The daughter volunteered to baby-sit the elderly grandmother who lived with them so that the parents could go out with peace of mind. The children also planned to clear the living room a couple of evenings that week so that the parents could watch television alone together.

Once the children finished their plan for the parents for the next week and it was all down in writing, the therapist brought the parents into the therapy room. She told them that she had explained to the children that the father's pain was a pain in his marriage and that the parents had forgotten how to be happy together, and therefore, she had put the children in charge of the parents' happiness. From then on, the parents were to follow the children's instructions, and the children would tell them what to do so that they could be happy again. She said that the children had prepared a list of the things the parents were to do in the next week, and they would now read it and explain it to the parents. The parents began to laugh as soon as the dinner was explained to them and, as the plan developed, they were clearly moved by their children's concern for them. The mother did not object since it was a plan made not by the therapist but by her wonderful children. The parents promised to follow all the instructions, and the session ended with the therapist congratulating them for having such wonderful children.

The family came back one week later, and the therapist

once more asked the children into the interview room alone.
They reported on how the plans had been carried out. The dinner had not gone quite as planned because they had neglected
to properly explain the situation to their older brother, who
had come home unexpectedly and eaten half the hamburgers
they had prepared for the parents. They also had not set the
table as well as they might have, so it was decided to repeat the
dinner but to do it better and with the collaboration of the
brother, to whom the therapist wrote a letter explaining the
plan. Everything else had gone well. The children made a similar
plan for the next two weeks, encouraged by the positive changes
that had occurred in the parents' mood and in the way they got
along together. This time they added a plan for the parents to
go out a couple of evenings together. The parents were called in,
and they confirmed the children's report and listened to their
instructions for the next two weeks. They were amused, and the
mood between them was better than in the previous sessions.
Then the children were asked to go to the waiting room so the
therapist could talk with the parents for a few minutes. The
parents reported improvement in their feelings for each other.
They also discussed with the therapist the father's decreased use
of drugs. (He had been going every day for court-ordered urine
testing, which was reported to the therapist, and his urine had
been clear of drugs since the beginning of the therapy—for the
first time in many years.)

The session two weeks later proceeded in a similar manner. The children reported first and made another plan for the
parents; then the parents came in, confirmed the children's report, listened to the new plan, agreed to follow it, and finally
talked for a few minutes alone with the therapist. The older
brother sent word to the therapist that he would follow his
younger siblings' instructions but that he now had a full-time
job and could not come to the sessions. The children's new
planned activities for the parents included a trip to a beach and
casino resort, birthday and anniversary celebrations, social
gatherings, and outings to the theater. The parents went gam-
bling, and the mother discovered that she enjoyed it a great
deal, which was good, because there was the implication that

she could also develop a vice. This was the first sign that she had an inclination to indulge in an activity that is not quite proper. The father was no longer the only one of the two who had such inclinations.

In the third month of therapy, the couple reported that they were quite happy together, but the wife said that she was still suspicious and that she could not forget the past. She was always looking for signs of the husband's previous addiction, looking in the old places where he used to hide his medication with the idea that she would find it again. The therapist suggested to the father that he leave love notes in those old hiding places so that, when the wife searched, not only would she not find the medicine but she would be reassured by the messages that her husband loved her.* The husband did this, and the wife's suspicions disappeared. She reported that she was pleased because the husband's behavior toward the children—and particularly toward the oldest son, with whom he had clashed most— had changed greatly. The father had had a long, fatherly talk with this son and had become more involved with him; the boy had quit using drugs, was saving his money, and had been accepted back into the Navy to complete his training.

The therapy proceeded in the same way for approximately six months. The father's urine remained clean, and he faced his charges, paid his fines, and did not have to serve a jail sentence. During this period, the middle son came one day to the session when he was visiting from the seminary. The therapist reported to him what the family had been doing and explained that now his younger brother and sister were in charge of the parents' happiness. This son had been the child most involved in helping the parents in the past, and the therapist had to ease him out of this position and ascertain that he would not interfere with the plans of his younger siblings. Also during this time, the daughter turned fifteen and blossomed into a very attractive young woman. To the surprise of therapist and supervisor, who had not noticed, the mother explained that the daughter had been born with a club foot and had had an opera-

*This intervention was suggested by Judith Mazza.

tion but had always remained clumsy and physically unsure of herself. She was also dyslexic and had always been afraid and ashamed of writing. Being in charge of the parents had raised her confidence, and now she was doing well in school, had a boyfriend, and was happy with herself physically and intellectually.

The therapy proceeded in the same manner until the last session, when the parents said that they now knew how to be happy together and no longer needed such close supervision from the children.

To summarize, the marital problems were solved by the children, who were put in charge of the parents' happiness. The children's authority was expressed through very concrete plans for what the parents were to do. The parents' relationship improved as a result of the children's instructions and also as the parents mirrored the good relationship and the competent interaction between brother and sister. The cross-generation coalition between mother and children against the father was broken as the children were put in charge of both parents, bringing them together at the same level. The father's addiction and delinquency were never addressed directly; they disappeared as his marital and family situation improved. He became a more competent father and was able to give his children and wife the guidance and support they needed. Moved by the children's concern and caring, the wife became more tolerant and understanding. The behavior of the two problem children improved, one as a result of the change in the father, the other as a result of the authority vested in her by the therapist.

The Boy Who Took Care of His Mother

A Protective Services worker referred a case of child abuse. He explained that the circumstances of the case were rather extreme. The mother, who was single and on welfare, had four sons—a five-year-old, seven-year-old twins, and a ten-year-old. All the children had difficulties but the main problems were the twins, who set fires. They had set many fires in the apartment and had set fire to a van in the street and to a baby in her crib when she was visiting. They were also encopretic and, besides soiling their pants, they would stuff their excrement into holes in the walls. They held urinating contests on the bed and sometimes urinated out the window. The worker said that although the mother was abusive this was understandable, given the behavior of the children, and Protective Services was sympathetic to her. All the children except the twins were from different fathers, and all the fathers had disappeared. The mother had had a boyfriend living in the home, but he had left because he could not tolerate the twins. When one of the twins, Robert, was a baby, he had had a fractured skull, which was considered the result of the mother's abuse. That had been one of a series of episodes. The mother had been a heroin addict but had overcome the addiction by turning to religion, and was off drugs and very involved with her church. Protective Services had assigned her a homemaker, who helped her take care of her apartment, and they were willing to provide a worker who would pick up the family members and drive them to the Family Therapy Institute and back for every session.

The problem of abuse presents special difficulties for a therapist, whose natural inclination is to tell the parent what to do in relation to the child and how to behave in responsible and caring ways. In terms of hierarchy, however, the problem is that the abusive parent is down in relation to the children because he does not behave like an adult, responsibly in charge of the children. Under such circumstances, telling the parent what to do puts him even further down in the hierarchy in relation to the children. If this happens, the therapist is working against the goal he is trying to accomplish: to have the parent in a superior position, caring responsibly for the children.

Related to the issue of hierarchy are two other issues having to do with punishment and rejection. In cases of abuse, there is a natural tendency to want to punish the parent. This is inappropriate, since the issue in the family is too much punitiveness. Also, the rejection the therapist naturally feels toward the abusive parent must be taken into account, and the supervisor must help the therapist elicit all that is good in the parent so that the therapist can feel sympathetic and therapy can be possible.

A fourth issue to consider in this case is the fact that the family had been under Protective Services for three years. It could be assumed that during that period numerous attempts had been made by intelligent people to influence the mother. There was no reason to believe that a new therapist would succeed where others had failed. However, a different approach, an indirect strategy, might be successful where direct methods were not.

Another issue the therapist had to consider in this case was what would be defined as the presenting problem. The mother's behavior was a problem, and so was the children's. The therapy needed to change both, but there were special difficulties. Addressing the mother's abuse directly would create a hierarchical problem in that the mother would be humiliated and lose even more power than she had already lost in relation to the children. Also, an antagonism between mother and therapist would develop that would be difficult to resolve. In contrast, if the children's behavior were defined as the problem, the mother's disturbing behavior could be indirectly corrected as she collaborated with the therapist in changing the children. It was decided that, from the very beginning of the therapy, the ostensible goal would be to change the children.

The question of love is always important in child abuse: Is it possible to discover and develop the love a mother feels for her children? If so, change is possible. The therapy had to be conducted in a framework of love, not of violence or punitiveness. The issue was not only how to arrange for the proper love and caring to go from mother to children but also to understand why the children behaved in such extreme ways. A good way of understanding the why of a behavior is to think about its consequences. In this family, even though the children's disruptive behavior caused the mother a great deal of pain, it also put her in contact with Protective Services workers, who helped her in many ways. They saw to it that she had food and the basic necessities, as well as medical care and psychotherapy; they provided someone intelligent and concerned with whom she could talk; they drove her wherever she had to go; and they even provided a homemaker to help her with the housework and with the children. For this mother, her contacts with Protective Services workers were her most important relationships with adults. If the children's disturbing behavior was helpful to the mother in this way, then it was clearly necessary to arrange a different way for them to be helpful.

Love and caring are shared within a family in a limited number of ways. In a single-parent nuclear family, a mother can love and take care of her children, the children can love and take care of their mother, or the children can love and take care of each other. In a disturbed family, the mother does not care appropriately for the children, and the children love and take care of the mother in covert, inappropriate ways. If the children can be moved to take care of the mother in loving, appropriate ways, the mother can be moved to respond to the children's love with equal concern and good feelings. A hierarchical reversal that orients the children toward expressing their love openly and helpfully can lead the mother to correct the hierarchy, accepting the children's love, responding in kind, and responsibly taking charge. Reversing the hierarchy became the main strategy in this case, and it would be carried out in steps.

First, there would be no mention of abuse; the therapist would not bring it up in any way. Second, the therapist would begin the first session by asking the mother what terrible things the twins were doing. A good part of the interview would be spent listening to the mother tell about the horrible behavior of the children. The therapist would make such comments as "horrible, horrible," and would express her sympathy with the mother's plight. In this way, the therapist not only would join the mother but would actually begin to feel some sympathy toward her.

Next, the therapist would talk with the mother about her loneliness and the fact that she had no one to help her and protect her. This would set the stage for the fourth step, in which the children would be set up as protectors of the mother. The therapist would arrange this by asking the mother to pretend during the session that she was very distressed, sad, lonely, and tearful, and to have the children embrace her and tell her that they loved her and would always protect her. If this went well, most of the session would consist of demonstrations of love and concern from the children toward the mother, which, it was hoped, would help the mother reciprocate. The therapy then would take place in a context of love and not of punitiveness.

The therapist started the first session by asking the four boys to sit on the floor of the therapy room with paper and drawing pencils because she wanted to talk to their mother. She said, "I hear terrible things about your twins; tell me what terrible things they do." The mother, a big, fat woman with a soft face, had come into the session with a magazine. She set it aside and began describing the behavior that the Protective Services worker had mentioned. She said, however, that the worst one was Robert. His twin brother, Gerald, just followed his example, and the other two were doing all right. She added to the list of problems that Robert beat up savagely on other children, particularly little ones. He also not only put his excrement in holes in the wall, but if the mother covered the holes, he would make them again and urinate in them. The therapist said, "Terrible, terrible. What other terrible things do they do?" The mother described more episodes of violence and the firesetting that was very dangerous. She told how he had set fire to the mother's niece when she was lying in bed.

By starting the interview asking about the terrible things the twins did, the therapist was defining the situation as one in which the children were the problem and not the mother; the abuse was not to be discussed. The mother knew she should not abuse her children. She had a trial pending, and many others had talked to her about how she should behave differently. It was useless to approach her in the same way. An indirect method, however, might succeed in influencing her.

The therapist asked the mother, "Who protects you, who takes care of you?" The mother said that sometimes the older son, Christian, helped her; but she said, "I have nobody; sometimes I have gotten so bad I wanted to cry." She said that her sister had told her to get rid of Robert, and Protective Services had offered to put him away. "But," she said, "I wanted to stick with him, but he hasn't changed." She explained how she had taken him to various psychiatrists but it had done no good. Then she again began to talk about Robert's horrible behavior and how he had been setting fires since he was two or three years old.

The therapist listened to all this and then said, "You know, Mrs. Jones, a mother's love is the greatest and strongest love in the whole world, but even that love can come to an end. I want to ask you—and I could tell by the way you were looking at him—do you still have love for Robert?" The mother answered that she did love him. "I could tell by the way you looked at him," said the therapist, "and I really admire you for that." The mother cried.

The therapist had uncovered the best aspect of the mother: the love that she still had for her child. The sequence of the interchange was important in bringing out the mother's good feelings for the child. The therapist first had to define Robert as a problem, then hear about all the terrible things he did, then bring up the mother's love in such a way that the mother could not deny it; then, finally, she could express her admiration for the mother for loving her child in spite of all. As a result, the mother felt understood and respected. She was also emotionally touched, and the context for change was set.

The therapist then told Robert to give his mother a big hug and a kiss. Robert hugged and kissed her for a long time, clinging to her while his five-year-old brother hovered around and tried to dry the mother's tears. The therapist moved the little one away and asked Robert to wipe the mother's eyes and say to her, "I'll take care of you. I promise I'll take care of you. I promise, Mama. I promise I'll take care of you." The child repeated the therapist's words very softly and hugged the mother for several minutes while the mother caressed him.

The therapist said, "From now on, you are going to be Mama's helper. You are going to be in charge of helping Mama have an easy life. Tell Mama one thing that you are going to do. You are in charge." The boy said very timidly, "Clean up." The therapist said, "You seal that bargain with a hug and a kiss." And they did. "One more thing as the in-charge person," said the therapist. "Be good," said Robert. The therapist said, "Seal that with a kiss, because from now on you are going to be in charge to see that things go well in your house for your mother.

What else?" "Behave in school," said Robert. "Seal it with a kiss," said the therapist.

Being happy would have seemed too far removed from reality for this mother to accept its possibility, but having an easy life was something that she could imagine, so Robert was put in charge not of her happiness but of helping her have an easy life. Since it had been so difficult for others to arrange the proper affect from the mother toward the child, the therapist arranged for the child to show the proper affect and responsibility toward the mother so that the mother could respond in kind. The mother responded with tears and showed a great deal of love for her child. She clung to him and did not let him go.

After a few minutes, the therapist asked Robert to sit in a chair facing the mother. She said to the mother, "Mrs. Jones, I want you to get really sad, like you get sometimes when it's awful, and I want you to talk like you do when you get sad. Say, 'I'm sad and lonely, nobody protects me, there's not enough food, there's not enough money, I don't know what I'm going to do.' And Robert, I want you to listen to Mama and tell me if she's doing it right."

The mother did as she was asked, and she began to sob as she spoke. She said that she was very lonely and that she had no one, unless she called her Protective Services worker. The therapist asked Robert to give the mother another big hug and a kiss and to tell her that he would always be there for her. The child did as he was told. Mother and son embraced, and the mother cried loudly as the therapist quieted the other children and kept the little one, who was constantly trying to get in the middle, from interfering.

The hypothesis behind this intervention was that Robert was very fond of and attached to the mother. His dreadful behavior was probably a reaction of despair to seeing his mother unhappy, lonely, and distraught. He gave her a focus for unhappiness that perhaps was more tolerable for her than was thinking about her other misfortunes. Through his misbehavior and by being a victim of abuse, the child had arranged for the mother the only contacts she had with people who helped her—the Protective Services workers. By making overt the mother's despair and her request for help, the child could help her in an appropriate way rather than with his destructive behavior. Because of the intense nature of the unfortunate relationship between mother and son, the therapist had to go even further and put the son in charge of the mother so that he could help her and so that she could receive the kind of love and caring she needed.

The therapist said, "During the next week, I want you to be together all the time when you are in the house, hugging and holding hands, because you both need a lot of love. Are there any chores you could do together?" The mother said that Robert always helped her clean and dust. In fact, he helped her more than the others. "That is why," she said, "it's so hard when people say 'put him in a place,' because any mother loves her children, and I love my son." The mother was now saying positive things about the child she had described as being so horrible at the beginning of the session.

The therapist said, "I can tell that you are right, and this is going to be your best son. This is going to be the son who takes care of you in your old age. You were right." In this way, the therapist increased the mother's positive feelings by implying that the mother had actually said that Robert was going to be her best son. The mother then talked about how she was afraid that Protective Services would take the child away from her, and the therapist had her tell Robert that no one would take him away, that she, the mother would not let them. This confirmed the mother in a protective, benevolent position and reassured the child.

Then the therapist said that since one big concern with Robert was safety, she wanted to play a little game. The mother was to show Robert in the session how to set a fire and how to put it out correctly, and Robert was to show the mother that he could do it. A can, paper, matches, and water were brought in, and the fires were set and put out while the other children watched in admiration and applauded.

The session ended with the therapist recommending that mother and son spend a lot of time together, hugging, holding hands, baking cookies, and that Robert set five fires a day for the next week under the mother's supervision.

After this session, all the major symptoms of the child disappeared, and there was no more abuse on the part of the mother. Robert did not set a fire again, the encopresis and enuresis disappeared, and he no longer was violent toward other children. Other, minor problems also were resolved in the therapy, which lasted approximately nine months with sessions every two or three weeks.

The second and third sessions were similar to the first, with the mother pretending to be sad and Robert embracing her and promising to take care of her and with mother and child practicing the firesetting. Later in the therapy, it was found that Robert was stealing lunches from other children at school. It was suspected that he did not get breakfast in the morning, so, instead of telling the mother that she should feed the children, the therapist arranged for the children to feed each other and the mother. She gave Robert an alarm clock, and he was put in charge of awakening the others in the morning and making sure that everybody made his or her bed. Then all the children would take turns making breakfast and serving it to each other and to the mother. Twice a week, the children would prepare dinner instead of the mother. The oldest son would be in charge of seeing that there was enough food in the house and of going to the store if necessary. The problem of stealing food was solved.

Other problems were solved in similar ways. All through the therapy the children were put in charge of resolving all problems, and little or nothing was asked of the mother. She responded as expected by becoming more responsible and taking care of the children.

At the beginning of the therapy, the mother was depressed and had a variety of health problems. By the end of the therapy, she was healthy, had lost a considerable amount of weight, and was active and cheerful. Her boyfriend, who had left her because he could not put up with the twins, came back to live with the family; and the children enjoyed him. The mother gave a talk to three hundred people at a church function on her experiences with Protective Services. The boys became involved in the church choir and enjoyed it. The mother accepted a job with Protective Services and was promoted to being in charge of the mail room. She left the house every morning at nine o'clock to go to work and came home when the children came back from school.

During the course of the therapy, numerous interventions had to be made in the school system, the medical system, and Protective Services to prevent agents from the community from intervening in well-intentioned but unfortunate ways. The family was living in the suburbs instead of in the black inner-city from which they had originally come; perhaps, had they stayed in the city, they would not have attracted so much attention from all kinds of helpers. The family pediatrician, for example, constantly undermined and threatened the mother and repeatedly called the school to communicate her concerns about Robert. It turned out that Robert had anemia, which had gone undetected and which probably explained the stealing of school lunches. This illness was used in the therapy to insist on a consultation with Children's Hospital; from there the family was referred to another pediatrician, which gave the mother a fresh start in dealing with a doctor who might not be so predisposed against her because of her previous history.

In terms of the school, the therapist communicated frequently with the teacher and appeared in court numerous times to keep Robert in the mainstream, counteracting the system's efforts to help the child by making him even more different and marginal through placements in special schools for the emotionally disturbed. Protective Services was supportive of this effort and was also able to gradually relinquish control of the mother.

The Mother Who Would Not Smile

A fifteen-year-old girl had been in therapy at the Family Therapy Institute for three years, which was an unusually long therapy. During this period, therapy had been terminated twice and then reactivated when problems developed, which occurred when the father rejected her and would not let her live with him. Several different therapists and supervisors had attempted to solve the problem. At the beginning of the therapy, the parents had been involved in a stormy divorce and the girl had been living with her father and grandmother; she had been torn between the father and the mother, who had the two younger siblings and who would have preferred to get back together with her husband. The mother then gained custody of all three children because the father did not want any of them. The struggle between the mother and father had made it difficult for the children to relate to the father. The girl had been hospitalized once prior to the therapy and once during the course of therapy. These hospitalizations were for suicide threats, running away, and disruptive behavior. During the first three years, most of the effort of therapy centered on negotiating issues of visitation and child support and on attempting to put the mother in charge of her daughter. The therapy was successful in terms of achieving peace between mother and father, but it failed in terms of putting the mother in charge of the daughter and improving the daughter's behavior.

In the fourth year of therapy, the author began to supervise the case. The therapist, who previously had been struggling with the family, had been attempting to help the mother enforce some rules and had been begging her to become involved in some adult activities, make friends, go out more, perhaps date. All his efforts had failed. The daughter was loud, rude, and impudent. The mother was devastating in her criticism of the girl and appeared totally rejecting of her. She clearly favored her eleven-year-old daughter and her five-year-old son. All the mother's concern for her oldest daughter, Andrea, seemed to be expressed only by her persistence in coming to the sessions.

Direct attempts over the years to put the mother in control and to make Andrea behave had not worked, and the bad feeling between mother and daughter had not diminished. It was difficult for the therapist even to conduct the sessions because of the way mother and daughter shouted at each other. A drastic change of strategy was needed. The supervisor instructed the therapist to ask Andrea whether she had noticed that her mother never smiled and that she was always serious and sad. Were she to advise her mother on how to have a happier life, what would she say to her? Andrea answered with hostility that

she didn't know and didn't care. The therapist said that he
knew how difficult it was to give the mother advice because she
refused to follow it; he had been trying to do just that for
months. However, he said, he was interested in hearing from
Andrea what she thought would be good advice for her mother.
The mother interrupted with some negative remark about how
Andrea was not qualified to give anyone advice, and the therapist answered that he would now appreciate it if the mother
remained quiet so that he could have a chance to talk with her
children. With a great deal of coaxing and suggestions from the
therapist, Andrea began to talk about how she would advise her
mother. She said the mother should make friends, go out more,
take care of herself. The younger sister, Janet, and the little
brother, Jimmy, began to participate in the conversation and
make suggestions. Pretty soon the conversation became ani-
mated and all three children were laughing about how the mother could find a date, the places she could go, and so on. The
therapist made some funny contributions, and the atmosphere
became happier than it had been in previous sessions. Through
all this, the mother sat impassive and without a smile on her
face. The session ended with the recommendation that the children should think of more advice that they could give the mother if she ever were to listen.

In the next session, the therapist began by asking the
mother about how things were going. He listened patiently for
five minutes to the mother's complaints about Andrea and then
asked her to let him talk to the children. He then proceeded, as
in the previous session, to discuss what advice the children
would give the mother if they could advise her. (It was important to use the conditional "if" because it was clear that the
mother would not accept anything from Andrea, especially advice.) A discussion with a great deal of laughter followed, as the
therapist suggested that perhaps the mother should take belly
dancing lessons and asked if the children would give her that advice. The mother showed a hint of a smile, but most of the time
she remained serious and grim.

From then on, all the sessions were conducted in the
same way. First, the therapist would listen to the mother's com-

plaints for two or three minutes, then he would spend most of the session discussing with the children what advice they would give her if they could give her advice. During several sessions, the children were asked to try to make the mother smile. They told jokes and stories, and finally the mother began to laugh. They were asked to surprise the mother with jokes at home to see if they could make her smile. A few sessions were devoted to a discussion of other ways, apart from telling jokes, to get the mother to smile—kind or happy things the children could do for her and for each other.

As the weeks went by, with sessions once or twice a month, Andrea began to behave more responsibly and maturely and to actually help her mother with the younger children and with the house. The therapist never devoted more than the first five minutes to listening to the mother's complaints. Andrea remained obnoxious and petulant, and it always took a while and some effort from the therapist to get her to talk. But in every session, eventually, the children would have a lively discussion about how to advise the mother, and the mother would sit listening to the children's advice and watching them and the therapist enjoy each other.

One day the mother said to the therapist that she understood that what he was doing was having good results, but it was difficult for her not to complain. She wanted to know if she could call him on the phone to complain to him. He said that that would be all right, and he began to call her once every two or three weeks to listen to her complaints. In the sessions, the therapist tied these complaints to the advice that the children gave the mother. Once, for example, when the mother complained about the nasty, impolite way in which Andrea talked, a session was dedicated to what advice the children would give the mother on how to talk like a lady. They had all seen My Fair Lady, and the therapist suggested that they make the mother say, "The rain in Spain stays mainly in the plain," properly, as in the movie. They did so, the mother collaborated, and, in the process, Andrea became more ladylike.

As Andrea improved, her sister, Janet, began to have problems with the mother. In one session, Janet complained bitterly about how the mother rejected her affection. She said that when the mother came home from work, she would approach her affectionately, and the mother would say, "Go away; don't bother me." Janet cried as she related this, Andrea comforted her, and there was more equality between the sisters in relation to the mother.

Andrea's improvement was steady but not without its ups and downs. As she stabilized in her new behaviors, the mother began to change. She smiled, laughed, and expressed appreciation for Andrea, whose help in the house and with the children was important. The mother was concerned about her daughter's sexuality, so in one session, to which the two came alone, the therapist asked them to pretend that the mother was the daughter and Andrea was the mother, and he asked Andrea to advise her daughter about sex. Andrea gave very mature, responsible advice, saying, for example, that a girl should always avoid finding herself in a situation in which she couldn't say "No." The mother was impressed, and they decided to take a sex education course together.

The therapy using this approach lasted a year with sessions every two or three weeks. During this time, Andrea and her mother developed a better relationship, the mother became considerably happier and more accepting, and Andrea's behavior improved. Janet and the little brother survived these changes without developing problems. In a follow-up interview a year after the therapy was terminated, Andrea's grades had improved from F's to C's and she was learning to drive. The mother expressed without reluctance her appreciation for Andrea's help in cleaning, cooking, and caring for the children. Mother and daughter were friendly and warm toward each other.

Conclusion

The three cases presented in this chapter are similar in that in all three a parent was incompetent, rejecting, symptomatic, or delinquent. They are different in that the presenting problems and the family members having the problems were different: In the first case, the father had the presenting prob-

lem; in the second case, both the mother and child had presenting problems; in the third case, the daughter had the presenting
problem. In all three cases, the children were the therapists, the
change agents. In the first case, the children were put in charge
of organizing the parents' lives so that they would be happy. In
the second case, the child was put in charge of seeing that the
mother would have an "easy life" and of initiating demonstrations of affection toward the mother. In the third case, the children were asked to say what they would suggest if they could
advise the mother. This approach can be used with a variety of
problems and family structures, regardless of the ages of the
children.*

---

*Another way of using family members as therapists can be found
in Landau-Stanton and others (1982).

4

Finding the Humorous Alternative

Humor, like all man's efforts to make sense of the world, involves the issue of classification. That is, an event can be classified as sad or amusing, boring or exciting, trivial or important, depending on the context that defines it. In therapy, this context develops from the interaction between the therapist and his clients. A therapist can create a humorous context to lessen his own power or authority or to help a client feel at ease or as part of the strategy to solve the presenting problem. A situation can be defined in various ways, just as the same story can be told as a comedy, a drama, a satire, a romance, or a mystery. Therapy often can be seen as an effort to change the genre: from drama to comedy of errors, from tragic romance to adventure story, and so on.

Victor Frankl (1960) and Milton Erickson (1954) were probably the first to introduce the idea of humor as a legitimate aspect of therapy. Frankl's technique of paradoxical intention involved asking a patient wishing to get over a symptom to deliberately try to have the symptom right there in the therapist's office. For example, if a patient were afraid of passing out, Frankl would ask him to try to pass out right there in the office. Frankl explained that a patient is usually perplexed by a request to deliberately suffer the symptom that he has come to therapy to resolve and laughs at the absurdity of the situation. This laughter is what Frankl was after. Frankl might not have been the first therapist to use paradox, but he appears to be the first to suggest that change is related to finding humor in the situation.

Humor often is found by an observer but not by the participants at that time. In his paper "Indirect Hypnotic Therapy of an Enurectic Couple," Erickson (1954) describes a young couple who consulted him because, shortly after their wedding, they discovered that they were both lifelong enurectics. Erickson instructed them to deliberately and simultaneously wet the bed every night for a period of two weeks and then to sleep on the wet bed. As a result of this directive, the involuntary bed wetting disappeared after the two-week period. It is doubtful that this instruction appeared humorous to the couple at the time that it was given, but Erickson writes that they were amused when they came back to report the results.

Humorous interventions often do not appear humorous to family members and clients. It is only in retrospect, after the problem has been solved and people have a more optimistic view of life, that the humor becomes apparent. The uniquely human characteristic of being able to laugh at one's own predicament seems to disappear when people are involved in serious conflicts and to be recovered as these conflicts are resolved.

Probably humor was being used by therapists for decades, but it was Frankl and Erickson who brought it out of the closet in professional publications. Today there are numerous publications that deal with the subject, and it is accepted in a variety of modalities of therapy.

A therapist can follow either of two broad approaches in using humor to change the context of a person or the drama of a family. One is based primarily on the use of language to redefine situations. The other relies on organizing actions that change a course of events and modify sequences of interaction. Some therapists prefer one or the other approach, but some, like Milton Erickson, are masters of both.

Talk*

Strategic therapy often involves changing the genre and can begin with a redefinition of the problem through the use of humor. For example, a thirty-year-old alcoholic refused to hold a job and lived with his parents, who were retired and ill and who were preoccupied with the young man and spent their time bickering about him. They described him as a bum, without either a goal in life or a career. The therapist said that the young man was not a bum and that he did have a career, but that his career was not recognized or socially acceptable in our culture. His career was to entertain his parents, to keep them busy and focused on him rather than picking on each other. Was he on an alcoholic binge? Had he gotten in trouble with the law? Had he found a job and then lost it? All these concerns kept the parents entertained and kept him involved with them. He was like the recreation director on a cruise ship, keeping the old people amused, and he really should be making a salary at this job instead of receiving only criticism. Perhaps if he were appreciated instead of only criticized, he would develop more interesting ways of entertaining his parents than getting drunk and raising hell. Maybe he would take them to a movie, on a picnic, or even to a museum and provide a wider variety of recreation for them.

The therapist, who was close in age to the young man, said that he, in fact, respected and admired the son for having chosen a career that goes against the cultural values of our time, does not lead to a good income or to a contribution in some area of endeavor, and is not conducive to marriage and children, the things most men want to have. The therapist added that he himself had chosen a career as a therapist (against the wishes of his father, who wanted him to be a banker) and that he was not nearly as devoted to his own parents as the young man was to his, since he saw them only occasionally. This was because he,

*The therapists in the examples presented in this chapter were: Richard Whiteside, M.S.W.; Joe Pastore, M.S.W.; Lyn Stycinski, Ph.D.; Bette Marcus, Ph.D.; Heidi Hsia, Ph.D.; June Kaufman, Ph.D.; Neil Schiff, Ph.D.; Frank Schindler, Ph.D.; Galen Alessi, Ph.D.; Judith Mazza, Ph.D.; and Patricia Davidge, M.S.W.

the therapist, had other interests; but, he remarked, since we are all different from one another, who is to say that one person's way is better than another's? Although the therapist's view was taken by the family as being more sarcastic than humorous, the young man improved and the parents went away on vacation for the first time in years. They said that if their son would not leave them, they would move to another state and leave *him*.

Language can be manipulated in infinite ways to be humorous and therapeutic. A middle-aged alcoholic was in therapy with an eager young man who was determined to cure him. The alcoholic was an expert at asking for help and then refusing to be helped, and he constantly complained about his problems while refusing to do anything to change his situation. He appeared to enjoy frustrating the young therapist, who responded to every rebuke with increased interest. The therapist was instructed to begin every statement he made during a session with the words, "I am not going to tell you," so that he would be negating what he would immediately say. The therapist said, for example: "I am not going to tell you that a man should not beat his wife." "I am not going to tell you that a man in your situation should be looking for a job." "I am not going to tell you that you should take care of your children." As the session progressed, the man became more and more irritated with the therapist, until finally the irritation turned to laughter and he began to ask, "What else are you not going to tell me?" By disqualifying his own statements in this way, the therapist was able to disengage from his intense involvement with the alcoholic and become more effective in influencing him.

Often the wisdom of popular humor lies in the fact that it forces us to realize that the unit is the system. For example, a favorite story about drivers is the one about the woman stalled in the middle of traffic. As she starts her car twenty times in a row only to have the engine die before she can move, a man behind her keeps blaring his horn, even though he can see her predicament. Finally, the woman gets out of her car, goes to the driver behind her, and says, "I'm awfully sorry, but I don't seem to be able to start my car. If you'll go up there and start it for me, I'll stay here and lean on your horn."* The humor in this story is similar to that in an intervention in which the therapist promises a wife that he will criticize her husband himself if the wife is nice to the husband. Since it is necessary for someone always to be critical of the man, the therapist will take on the job and free the wife for a more pleasant interaction. In this case, as well as in the story about the drivers, the unit is a dyadic pair that is working together to maintain the status quo. Many techniques of therapy are similar to the punch line of a joke, as the punch line is so often the truth about interpersonal relationships. Wife and therapist can change positions, just as the two drivers can change positions, leading to humor. Changing positions is similar to taking turns, a form of cooperation highly valued in our culture. Sharing an unfortunate position by taking turns at causing distress is both humorous and therapeutic (see the case of The Life Ruiner in Chapter Two).

Another approach that involves changing positions has to do with changing the perspective of a person in a family. A young couple consulted for divorce counseling when their divorce was about to become final. The husband was twenty-two years old and had an unstable job history. The wife was twenty-six and had married him when she accidentally became pregnant. At the time of her marriage, the wife's father had recently died and she was living with her mother, who was trying to overcome her depression. The two women had decided that it would be nice to have a baby. The grandmother went to work to support her daughter and grandchild. Both women excluded the young man, who alternated between brave attempts to become a responsible breadwinner and aimless wanderings across the country. The wife sued for divorce, which was about to become final when the baby was two years old.

The couple came for divorce counseling to negotiate visitation and to improve communication so they could deal better with the child. However, the husband had the secret agenda of

*This story, as well as several others in this chapter, were taken from Ralph Marquard, *Jokes and Anecdotes for All Occasions*, 1977.

getting back together with his wife. In the second session, the husband's wishes were made explicit and the wife made it very clear that she would not go back with him. Before the third session, the divorce became final. During that week, the husband unexpectedly appeared at the wife's house and demanded to be driven somewhere. The wife refused, and the husband took a knife and slit his arms longitudinally, shouting, "This will give you pleasure!" Then he grabbed the baby and ran down the street. The wife caught up with him and took him to the emergency room, where he got some stitches.

After this crisis, all available family members were invited to the next session. The young man, the wife, the baby, an uncle of the young man, and the young man's father, who came from another state, were present. The grandmother did not arrive until the session was over. The young man appeared depressed and humiliated. The therapist asked each person how he or she thought this kind of dangerous act by the young man could be prevented in the future. The wife and the young man said that surely he must be mentally ill. The father and the uncle said that the young couple had made a mistake in continuing to see each other when they were separated, that there should have been a cooling-off period with more distance between them. It sounded to the supervisor as if the two older men were right and the therapeutic error had been not to arrange for this distance. A strategy was planned to correct the mistake.

The therapist asked the young wife to leave the room with the baby because the therapist wanted to speak to the men alone. She then told the father and uncle that what the young husband needed was an attractive, strong young woman on his side to counteract the power of the ex-wife and her mother. He needed a woman with whom he could enjoy having sex and who would be jealous about and possessive of him. It was the duty of the father and uncle to help the young man find such a woman, since he obviously was not willing to do it by himself; otherwise, such a handsome young man as he would be involved with a woman already. In fact, he was probably occupied in fighting them off. Therefore, right after the session the father and uncle had to take the young man out on the town to pick up a girl, or at least to meet women. The three men laughed, and the atmosphere of the session turned to something similar to that of a bachelor party. The young man said that he did not need help and could pick up a girl by himself quite well. The therapist would not hear of it. The father and uncle said that they both were married and their wives would not look favorably on this idea. The therapist said that she understood that this was a sacrifice she was asking of them and of their wives, and they would have to explain to their spouses that this had been a therapeutic recommendation. In fact, the therapist would be happy to write letters to the wives explaining the situation. Stroking their moustaches, father and uncle said that they would just have to sacrifice themselves and go out looking for girls. There was a great deal of joking and laughter as they planned where they would go. The young man forgot his depression and participated actively in the discussion, suggesting which would be the better places. The therapist said that that night would be just the beginning. From then on, father and uncle had to collaborate in finding women for the young man until he was involved in a sexual relationship with a strong, beautiful woman who would protect him from his ex-wife and her mother. There was more laughter, and the uncle suggested that attractive women could be found in places other than night spots—for example, in church. The idea was accepted, and further plans were made. The session ended with the three men taking off for a night on the town.

From then on, the sessions involved only the three men and had the same focus: the father and uncle were to advise the young man and help him find women. The father was put in charge of all decisions with regard to his son's life, and it was decided that there would be no visits to the ex-wife until he was involved with another woman. Arranging for this involvement was not an easy task. There were ups and downs, and it took more than two months for the young man to begin to have sexual relations with other women. Other issues were dealt with in various ways, and the ex-wife and grandmother were seen separately. The mood, however, remained changed. The humorous directive of asking the father and uncle to sacrifice themselves by helping the young man find women changed the focus of the therapy. Instead of dealing with mental illness, depression, loss, and separation, the theme of the therapy was fun and sex.

The humor in a story often consists of some kind of reframing or relabeling of a situation. For example, in the midst of a heated argument, a wife began beating her diminutive husband. In terror he ran into the bedroom and crawled under the bed. "Come out!" she cried. "No!" he shouted back from under the bed. "I'll show you who's boss in this house!"

In therapy, it is often useful to relabel the weak as powerful and the powerful as weak, and the truth is always a matter of interpretation. A young, beautiful wife was always cutting down and rejecting her husband while complaining that he was inhibited and did not express himself or communicate his feelings as she expected. The husband kept apologizing but defending his need to spend long hours at his office involved with his promising career. The therapist told the wife that, in fact, her criticism and rejection of the husband were extremely kindly to him, since he probably could not tolerate having a loving wife. He had not received enough love and caring from his father during his childhood (the husband had talked about this in therapy), and therefore he was not prepared to receive the love of which he had been so badly deprived from anyone—particularly not from a beautiful wife whom he loved. If she was not critical and rejecting, if she were loving and devoted to him, he would be overwhelmed, might not be able to tolerate her affection, and might even leave her. Her rejection was really a manifestation of love that the husband should appreciate, because it was a way of staying close to him in a fashion that he could tolerate. The therapist said that she would work to improve the couple's relationship but that the wife must always maintain a certain level of rejection so that the husband would not get upset; the therapist did not want to improve the relationship to the point that the husband would leave the wife. For several weeks, the couple discussed in therapy what they could do to have more fun with each other and to have a better marriage, but always the therapist reminded the wife to be rejecting; and every session began with the therapist asking the couple whether the wife had been sufficiently rejecting since the last session. As a result, the wife became considerably less rejecting and the husband much more tolerant of having a loving wife.

A young man who was struggling to become an opera singer was referred to therapy by his voice teacher, who thought he could not reach certain notes because of emotional difficulties. The young man was in his mid-twenties, lived with his parents, held a menial job even though he had a college degree, and struggled to improve his singing. He spent a great deal of time keeping his mother company and was distant from his father, an engineer who was not sympathetic to the son's artistic vocation. The young man's difficulty in singing was solved in two sessions by asking him to deliberately make two mistakes: one that his teacher would notice and one that she would have trouble perceiving. As the young man struggled to make these mistakes, his skill improved, and he reached the notes that had presented difficulties. He said to the therapist, however, that his main reasons for coming to therapy were that he wanted to improve his relationship with his father and that he wanted his father to appreciate him. The therapist, a young, attractive, exotic-looking woman, said that she found his concern about his relationship with his father extremely interesting because it was so unusual. The young man asked why it was unusual, and the therapist answered that most young men in therapy these days are concerned with other things, so she had not had the chance to work with one who was mainly concerned about his father. She found this very moving and, although she did not know whether she could help him, she was certainly interested in the therapy because it would be a new learning experience for her. The young man asked what things other young men were concerned about, and the therapist answered: "Oh, mainly having more sex and making more money. That is mainly what they want, and it is not half as interesting as your problem of improving your relationship with your father and getting him to appreciate you." The young man said that he, too, wanted to have more sex and make more money; in fact, he would like to spend some time talking about that. The therapist said she knew that that was not so and that he was mainly concerned about his father; what was so fascinating to her was that this was such an old-fashioned problem. Young men many years ago had brought that problem to therapy quite frequently, but nobody at the institute had heard of a young man having that problem in recent years. The problem was so old-fashioned that it could not have even been the subject of an Italian opera—only of a German opera, because they were more boring. In fact, what the young man should do was write a German opera about a young man who wants to be appreciated by his father. There was a discussion of how such a story could go, the vicissitudes of such a young man, and how he would finally be appreciated by his father after a long life of suffering.* The young man agreed to write the German opera, then actually wrote it and read it to the therapist. As he was working on it, his interest in his father diminished and his interest in sex and money increased.

In relation to these new interests, it became apparent that there were no women in his life at all. He talked about his difficulty in finding a girl he liked and in approaching such a young woman. The therapist said that that was not his difficulty at all. His difficulty had to do with tolerating rejection. Because it was so difficult for him to tolerate rejection, he could not approach women for fear of being rejected. Therefore, what he had to do was practice feeling rejected. For this purpose, he had to stand at a certain corner in front of a certain boutique and spend several hours during two weekends inviting women to have a cup of coffee with him. They would refuse and he would have the experience of being rejected and tolerating it. Surprisingly, so many women accepted the invitation that the young man did not really have the chance to experience rejection.

As he began to feel more comfortable with women, the young man explained that one of his fears had always been that he would be taken for a homosexual. Because of his work in the theater, he thought that he had certain mannerisms that could be thought of as being effeminate. The therapist told him that that presented a wonderful opportunity and that he should practice leading a woman to believe that he was gay and then

*This approach was suggested by Claudio Madanes.

unexpectedly seducing her. The young man said that, in fact, he had already had that experience. Once he and a friend, after unsuccessfully trying to find girls at a beach resort, had pretended to be homosexual and had been very successful at convincing two girls to go out with them. The therapist said that she had not realized that he had such a range and that it would be difficult to arrange for experiences of rejection for him.

The therapy ended when the young man became involved with a girl who was very interested in sex. He then had to find a better job so he could move out of his parents' house and have some privacy with her. By this time, he had lost interest in whether his father really appreciated him. His concern about his father, his difficulties with women, and his fear of homosexuality had all been reframed in humorous ways that led to change.

The presentation of authority as fallible is a typical humorous device. Jokes abound about God, the Pope, the president, and so on. Some difficult problems of young people involve rebellious acts against a parent who is seen by the young person (accurately or inaccurately) as being extremely powerful. The positions in the family appear rigidly established: The parent attempts to take charge of the young person and fails, the young person refuses to obey the parent, and the war escalates with each confrontation. Reversing the hierarchy is a way of introducing humor, optimism, and the possibility of negotiation (see the cases of The Mother Who Would Not Smile and The Father With a Pain in his Marriage in Chapter Three).

Not only in therapeutic interventions but also in interviewing technique, there is a parallel between popular humor and therapy. Take the story of the young man who is going on his first blind date and is nervous about not having anything to say. His brother advises him, giving him a formula that never fails: talk about family, food, or philosophy. Any of those topics is guaranteed to get a girl talking. So the young man goes to meet the girl, who is pretty and shy. Eager to make a good impression, he follows his brother's advice and begins to talk about family. "Tell me, do you have a brother?" he says. "No," she answers. So he moves to the topic of food. "Do you like noodles?" "No," she says again. So the young man remembers his brother's advice. He'll talk philosophy. "Tell me," he says, "if you had a brother, would he like noodles?"

As in this story, in therapy it is often necessary to ask questions about apparently unrelated subjects in order to obtain information on which to base a hypothesis for change. When these questions are combined with a request to one family member to comment upon the relationship of two others (Selvini Palazzoli, Cecchin, Prata, and Boscolo, 1978), the effect is often humorous: "If your mother and your wife were to talk about your job, would they agree that you should strive for a better position?" "If your husband and your son were to talk about you, what would they say?" "If your daughter were worried about you, what would she be worried about?" "Would your wife be worried about the same thing as your daughter, or would she worry about something else?" Such hypothetical questions, which address issues between two or three people that might not have been addressed explicitly before, are the kinds of questions that lead to information about metaphor, planning, and hierarchy. The more guarded and reserved the family, the more humorous and off-the-wall the questions appear. However, as soon as an important issue is addressed, the questions no longer seem absurd or humorous.

Action

Slapstick is a form of humor that involves actions often mocking violence. It is sometimes used in therapy as a way of redefining a situation through actions rather than through verbal statements. A couple in their sixties consulted because of marital unhappiness. One of their problems was the wife's complaint that the husband became irritated by what she considered to be her idiosyncrasies, which he should accept benevolently. One such idiosyncrasy was her habit of doing things quickly and walking fast so that he could not catch up with her. For example, she would hand him a cup of coffee and drop it on the floor before he could grab it. They would get out of the car to go to a movie, and she would rush ahead of him in a way that he considered rude. She was asked to show how she walked fast in the session, and she jumped out of her chair and sprinted toward the door. She was asked to do this once more, and this time the husband was to run after her, grab her, and give her a big Rudolf Valentino-style kiss. The couple did this with much laughter. They were asked to practice this scene during the next week. The wife was to purposefully run away from the husband, and the husband was to grab her and kiss her dramatically, whether they were with friends, in the middle of the street, in a restaurant, or whatever. The slapstick routine counteracted the irritation and resentment of the couple's interaction, and the humor freed them to try new ways of relating.

It is not uncommon, when humor is used in therapy, for a family member to attempt to establish a secret coalition with the therapist. This is usually conveyed by nonverbal means, through a certain look out of the corner of the eye and a certain smile, twisted to one side, that implies that the therapist and that person are together in pulling the leg of another family member. In the previous example, when the husband was asked to act like Rudolf Valentino, he said with a wink and a smile that he did not know who Rudolf Valentino was and had never seen that type of kiss, implying that he was too young to know. The implication was that the therapist and he would humorously coax the wife out of her bad habit, while, in fact, the therapist's plan was to change both their behaviors.

It has been said that in all humor there is an element of defiance, be it of authority, socially accepted norms, or rules. Defiance can be used in ways that are not only humorous but therapeutic as antagonism is changed into playful challenge. Penn (1982) describes a technique to be used with young couples who may present marital, sexual, or communication difficulties and whose situation can be understood as resulting from the couple's difficulty in establishing a boundary around their relationship and protecting it from intrusions by and overinvolvement with in-laws. The couple is asked to visit both sets of in-laws; during these visits, the wife is to be overtly and exaggeratedly affectionate to the husband, holding his hand, whispering in his ear, kissing him, giggling, sitting on his lap. The husband is to respond by showing that he is pleased but shy and not reject-ing. The couple is then to go home and make notes of the be-havior they observed in the older couple as they performed their parts. Usually the in-laws send the couple home early, since it becomes clear that they have something going on be-tween them from which the older couple is excluded. The young couple can separate more easily from their parents through playful defiance than through unfortunate confronta-tions. The same approach can be used when one of the spouses is involved in conflictual ways with siblings, friends, or other relatives.

Not only defiance but also violence can be turned to a hu-morous encounter in a variety of ways. One young couple con-sulted because of the fighting and violence in their marriage. They described a sequence in which the wife would criticize the husband, he would withdraw, she would pursue him, and, even-tually, in frustration at his silence, she would start hitting him; to her shock, he would hit her back, sometimes quite painfully. They were both attractive, intelligent, and successful, but they could not change this interaction, which made them unhappy, horrified them, and prevented them from deciding to have chil-dren. The therapist conducted a long session exploring the con-sequences a happy relationship would have for both their ex-tended families and asked them to think further about those issues. Then he suggested that, in the next two weeks, every time the wife provoked the husband's anger, and particularly when she hit him, the husband, instead of hitting her back, should put his hand up her skirt or under her blouse and fondle her. Some of their fights had been in public, so this behavior would also take place even if it had to be in public. The couple laughed and agreed to do this. The directive was repeated for six weeks, and the violence and fighting disappeared. However, the husband said that, although they had not had the opportu-nity to follow the directive because there had been no fights or provocations, he had had opportunity to fondle his wife in dif-ferent circumstances. Therapy was terminated after two months; the couple had decided to have a baby and the wife thought she was already pregnant.

Often a story is humorous due to an incongruity between a situation and the framework in which it takes place. Woody Allen, for example, a masterful humorist, depends in many of his characterizations on the incongruity between two factors: his alleged prowess as a lover and his mousey physical appearance. As a writer, he also works on the humorous aspects of incongruities. In "The Stolen Gem," a satire on detective fiction, a character says "The sapphire was originally owned by a sultan who died under mysterious circumstances when a hand reached out of a bowl of soup he was eating and strangled him" (Allen, 1981, p. 21).

The element of incongruity is common both to humor and to paradoxical directives. A couple consulted about their twelve-year-old son, who had been setting fires for seven years. This activity endangered the father's job, because he worked for the government in situations in which he and his family repeatedly needed to obtain security clearance; this clearance was in jeopardy because of the child's firesetting. In fact, at an army party, the boy had set fire to explosives, an event that had driven the father to distraction. The mother could not leave the child alone in the house for five minutes for fear that he would burn it down. The father worked long hours and had little contact with the son. In the first session, the therapist had the boy demonstrate how he set a fire to see if he could do it properly. For this purpose a coffee can, papers, matches, and water were brought into the room. When the boy set the fire and put it out, the therapist criticized him severely, saying that he did not know the first thing about fires. He had not closed the match box; he had set the fire too close to the edge of the can so that a paper could have floated out and burned him; after pouring water in the can, he had put one hand inside too soon while touching the hot can with his other hand, and either hand could have been burned. All this, said the therapist, proved that the boy was completely incompetent about fires, and the irony was that he claimed to be an expert, judging from all the fires he had set. When the therapist left the room for a moment to empty the coffee can, the boy, who had listened to the therapist's harangue incredulously, said to his parents: "This guy is crazy." The therapist came back and asked the father to demonstrate for the son how to set and put out a fire correctly. Then he told the father that he needed to spend more time with his son in a fatherly way—and what better way than to spend time teaching the boy about fires as he had done in the session? He was directed to supervise the boy in this endeavor, setting a variety of fires with different materials in different places and putting them out. Father and son were to do this six times a day every day. The mother was to keep notes on their activities. The parents complied and carried out the task for several weeks. Sometimes the father, because of his long working hours and difficult schedule, had to awaken the son in the middle of the night to set a fire. On several occasions, the indignant child said that the therapist was crazy, and on occasion the parents seemed to think the same. The spontaneous firesetting, however, stopped immediately, and soon the boy asked whether he and his father could spend the time in more constructive ways than setting fires. Eventually, the therapist consented to this suggestion, and father and son discovered common interests and enjoyed each other. The directive to set fires was incongruous in the context of a therapy designed to end the firesetting. The father was asked to encourage the son to set supervised fires rather than not to set fires at all.* The ordeal of setting fires, first in the session and then several times a day to the point of having to get out of bed to set a fire in the middle of the night, the therapist's criticism of the boy as an inadequate firesetter, and the child's indignation at the therapist were humorous. In fact, the child was so provoked that he set out to demonstrate to the therapist that he was competent in all areas, and his grades in school improved remarkably. There was a quality of the absurd in the therapist's directives. This element of ridicule is common to humor and to paradoxical directives.

An element of incongruity often is also useful in training therapists. Haley (1983) tells about his approach to a very shy

---

*This approach was inspired by Braulio Montalvo, who used a similar intervention to bring a mother and daughter closer together. For other cases of firesetters, see Montalvo, 1973, and Madanes, 1981b.

student, who was terrified of Haley's supervision behind the one-way mirror. He instructed her to go into the therapy room to interview a family and to be sure to properly make three mistakes. Two of these mistakes would be obvious, and one mistake would be one that would not be evident to Haley. The student conducted the interview and after a while came out of the room to discuss the problem with Haley. He asked, "Did you make the three mistakes correctly?" She answered, "Screw you!" and was no longer overconcerned about his opinion. It is incongruous to ask a therapist to make mistakes properly in the context of teaching how to do therapy properly.

A therapist under supervision was a professor of behavior modification and was very concerned with telling people just what they should be doing. He had a difficult case of a little girl referred by her school for a variety of problems. She had been adopted by her grandparents after being abandoned by her mother. The therapist was instructed to deal with all problems by only saying to the grandparents, "I am curious to see how you will resolve that." This made sense in terms of increasing the grandparents' confidence as parents, but it was not the kind of directive approach the therapist was expecting to learn. However, he struggled to follow the supervisor's instructions, and the problems of lying, failing in school, and thumb sucking were dealt with only by saying, "I am curious to see how you will resolve that." The grandparents benevolently resolved all problems in a couple of months, and both the school and the therapist were impressed. Asking a student to make mistakes deliberately or to refrain from giving any directives is incongruent in the context of a directive therapy, in which the student is interested in learning how to give directives properly. However, just as with clients, it is usually only later that the student sees the humor in the situation.

An understatement of a problem can lead to humorous directives. A compulsive vomiter came to therapy after seventeen years of bulimarexia, which had resulted in the loss of all her teeth, various somatic problems, and years of unsuccessful therapy (see Chapter Five). The therapist told her and her family that what she was doing was simply throwing away food by mushing it up in her stomach first and then throwing it into the toilet. Why not mush up the food with her hands instead and place it in the toilet directly? This would be less harmful to her body than having the stomach do the work. The family was to provide the food and supervise the process. Saying that seventeen years of compulsive vomiting was simply throwing away food by passing it through the stomach first was an understatement of a severe self-destructive compulsion. The instructions were followed, however, and the vomiting disappeared eventually as a result of this and other paradoxical interventions.

A common element in popular humor and in strategic therapy is an ordeal designed to solve a problem, as in the cases of the firesetter and the compulsive vomiter. Take the story of the man who complains to the doctor about his uncontrollable cough. The doctor gives him a bottle of castor oil and tells him to go home, drink the whole bottle, and come back the next day. When he comes back, the doctor asks, "Did you drink the castor oil?" "Yes," says the man. "Do you still cough?" "Yes." The doctor gives him a second bottle of castor oil and tells him to drink it and come back the next day. The man follows the instructions and reports the next day that he is still coughing regularly. The doctor gives him yet another bottle and repeats the instructions. When the patient returns, the doctor asks, "Do you cough now?" The patient answers quiveringly, "I don't cough anymore. I'm afraid to."

This story is reminiscent of the ordeals often prescribed by Erickson to his patients (Haley, 1963). An old man complained that he could not sleep at night. He said that he only slept two hours even if he took sleeping pills and that his physician was worried about the amount of medication he was taking. Erickson found that the man, who lived alone with his son, felt he should do more housework, particularly waxing the floors, but he hated the smell of the wax. Erickson said to him, "I can cure you of your insomnia if you are willing to give up eight hours sleep." The man said that he was willing to make that sacrifice. Erickson told him that he should get ready for bed that night and put on his pajamas at his usual time, eight o'clock; but instead of going to bed, he was to wax the floor all night. At seven the next morning, he was to get dressed, have breakfast, and go to work as usual. The next night he was to repeat the procedure and polish the floors all night. He was to do this for four consecutive nights. Since he only slept two hours a night anyway, this only meant giving up eight hours sleep. The man went home and polished the floors for three nights. The fourth night he decided to lie down and rest his eyes for just half an hour. He awakened at seven the following morning. The next night he decided to go to bed at eight o'clock, and, if he could read the clock fifteen minutes later, he would get up and polish the floors all night. A year later he was still sleeping soundly every night; he did not dare suffer insomnia for fear of having to spend the night polishing floors. Erickson says, "You know the old gentleman would do anything to get out of polishing the floors—even sleep" (p. 49).

The author used a similar approach in the case of a woman who was a compulsive cleaner. She lived with her second husband and her daughter from a first marriage. The symptom had developed when she remarried and quit her job. She cleaned the house and everything in it constantly and compulsively. It took her hours to clean the kitchen after each meal and, to avoid the cleaning, her cooking was simple and uninteresting. Often her husband would bring home take-out food to prevent her from having to wash and clean the kitchen for hours after cooking a meal. Frequently, she had to get up in the middle of the night because she thought that somebody might have used a towel in the bathroom and she had to put it in the washing machine immediately. This aspect of her habit was particularly annoying to the husband, because the noise of the washing machine prevented him from sleeping. The woman did not have this problem when she visited her mother's house, which she did regularly, or other people's houses, nor did she have this problem in hotel rooms when the couple went on vacation. At home, however, the husband would sit by himself every evening and read the newspaper or watch television; then he would go to bed and continue watching television by himself, eventually falling asleep alone while the wife was still busy cleaning. He was twenty years older than the wife and, although he said that he

cared about his wife and wanted to help her, he was very disagreeable and obnoxious to the therapist, insisting that he did
not want to participate, that this was her individual problem to
solve. He was somewhat annoyed at having paid for five years of
psychoanalysis and for behavior modification and several experiences of the encounter and growth variety without results.
The husband also objected to the fact that the couple had to
drive two hours to come to the sessions. Obviously, the therapy
would have to be extremely brief if it were to involve the husband.

A humorous ordeal is particularly appropriate to brief
therapy and might succeed where other approaches have failed.
Given the information provided in the first interview, it was
postulated that the wife spent her time cleaning compulsively to
avoid being with her husband. If this were so, it would follow
logically that, if the consequence for exaggerated cleaning
would be for the wife to have to be closer to her husband, then
the situation would be reversed and she would clean less in
order to avoid him. Based on this hypothesis, the therapist gave
the couple two directives: a short-term intervention designed to
introduce an element of playfulness into the relationship and
a long-term recommendation that could continue to be effective
without a continuing therapeutic involvement.

The first intervention was to tell the couple that every
day for the following two weeks the wife would purposefully
leave something in the house uncleaned. When the husband
came home in the evening, he would search the house and try
to discover what it was that she had not cleaned that day. If he
discovered it, he would win and she would make dinner for him
as usual. If he lost, he would take her out to dinner. However,
it was important to ensure the wife's truthfulness; for this purpose, before the husband came home, she was to record the
item that she had not cleaned on a little slip of paper and stick
the paper in her bra between her breasts. The husband had to
find out whether he had won or lost by finding the slip of paper
and reading it. In this way, the problem of compulsive cleaning
would lead to the husband's fondling of the woman's breasts.
This was a daring directive to give to a couple that was quite

rigid and unimaginative. However, even though they might not follow the suggestion, the mere giving of the directive had introduced playfulness and sexual connotations into the situation. During those two weeks, the wife also was to make a detailed description of her cleaning and keep a log of the time she spent at it to use as a baseline for the next intervention.

In the next interview, the third, the husband said that he understood that the therapist wanted him to take a firmer position in relation to his wife and that he was planning to do just that. He had searched the house, failed to discover what she had not cleaned, and found the slip of paper a few times; he had not done this every day, but the couple had frequently gone out to dinner. The therapist reviewed the time log that the wife had brought to the session and proposed the following to the couple: A housekeeper works eight hours a day; the wife was working now as a housewife and housekeeper since she had quit her job; therefore, it would be normal for her to clean eight hours a day, but no more than that, as any hired housekeeper would. The husband said that only five hours a day of cleaning could possibly be necessary, but the couple finally agreed on eight hours of cleaning during the week and two hours on weekends and holidays, as would be normal for a housekeeper. The wife said that that would be normal for another woman but not for her.

Then the therapist said that she had a cure and that if the couple followed her instructions the problem of compulsive cleaning would be solved—but they had to promise to follow her directive before she would tell them what it was. The couple refused to promise, so the therapist gave them the directive anyway. Every day the wife was to stop cleaning at five o'clock (she had reported that she never started before nine). She then would shower and dress to look nice for her husband. When he came home, there would be no more cleaning; the wife instead could read, needlepoint, or do whatever she liked. She was only allowed half an hour to do the dishes after dinner. If she spent any time cleaning beyond that, the husband would force her to get into bed with him to watch television (which was what he enjoyed doing in the evening), and she would have to stay in bed with him until they fell asleep. If the husband preferred, instead of watching television together in bed, the punishment that he could enforce would be that the two would go out together either that evening or the next. The wife said that this would not work, and the husband said, "Excellent, I understand, excellent!" He commented that he had known all along that he should have taken a firmer position with her and that for this it was not worthwhile to come to therapy.

With this the couple terminated the therapy. They were followed up with phone calls every three months for the next nine months, and they reported that the wife was cleaning only from nine to five and for only two hours on weekends. Some days she preferred to go out and did not clean at all. However, the wife emphasized, the improvement had nothing to do with the therapy.

In the case of the insomniac, Erickson knew that the man thought that he should wax the floors but did not want to do it. In the case of the compulsive cleaner, it was suspected that the woman thought she should spend more time with her husband but did not want to do it. The case of the insomniac is most similar to the story of the man with the cough in that in both cases a worse alternative to the symptom is offered (castor oil and waxing floors). In the case of the compulsive cleaner, a worse alternative is also offered (to get into bed with the husband or to go out with him); but this alternative is precisely the one behind the symptom—the one that, in the therapist's view, the woman had construed the symptom in order to avoid. She could not be with her husband because she had to clean. The therapist turned cause and effect around and proposed that if she cleaned she had to be with her husband. The purpose of the symptom was defeated.

Passing the ball is a well-known theory of mental health. If anything upsets you, you should immediately tell your story to others until you find someone who is willing to be more upset about it than you are. At that moment, you will feel good once again and be able to go about your business. Often a therapeutic intervention consists of arranging to pass the ball, as in taking turns (see the case of The Life Ruiner in Chapter Two).

Sometimes, however, the same goal can be accomplished with a contract. For instance, when a single mother and her son agree that every time the son brings home an A the mother will go out on a date, the problem has been passed to the mother. The problem has become the mother's loneliness rather than the son's academic difficulties (see Chapter Five). When an anorectic agrees that if the father does not drink she will eat, but if the father drinks she will starve herself, the ball has been passed to the father and his alcoholism becomes the issue (see Chapter Five). The humorous effect of these approaches is related to passing the ball, but the therapeutic effect consists of solving the original problem that was expressed through the symptomatic behavior, which was itself a misguided attempt at a solution (in the case of the student, the child's concern about the mother's loneliness; in the case of the anorectic, the anorectic's concern about her father's alcoholism).

The Therapist

Humorous interventions in therapy include an element of surprise, of the unexpected. A humorous redefinition, explanation, or directive takes the family by surprise in a way that gives strength, drama, and impact to the intervention. Humor often allows the therapist's creativity to match the creativity of the symptom. To have impact a therapist must have the ability to tolerate ridicule, to appear absurd, to risk loss of face, since sometimes the laughs turn on the therapist in unexpected ways. Humor should not be confused with sarcasm, however. It is therapeutic to laugh with the client, not at the client. It is better for a therapist to ridicule himself than a patient or a family.

What makes change possible is the therapist's ability to be optimistic and to see what is funny or appealing in a grim situation. Humor involves the ability to think at multiple levels and in this way is similar to metaphorical communication. When a therapist talks about a meal or a game in tennis in ways that are metaphorical of a sexual relationship, the humorous aspect of the communication becomes apparent as soon as the connection is made between the two levels. Thinking at multiple levels also involves the ability to be inconsistent, to be illogical, and to communicate in non sequiturs, jumping from one subject to another, associating what seems to be unrelated in ways that appear humorous and are therapeutic. In order to use humor in therapy, the therapist must have a sense of humor, whether or not the client does.

5

Choosing
the Right Strategy

A strategic therapist must have a strategy. The issue is choosing
the strategy that is best suited to each different kind of problem. Traditional diagnostic categories are not helpful in making
this choice. A therapist must develop the right thoughts so that
he can not only come up with the right intervention but also
elicit in himself the sympathy for and interest in the clients that
will make it possible to influence them. What makes a therapist
choose a particular strategy is how he conceptualizes a problem
brought to therapy as well as the specific characteristics of the
problem itself or of the people who present it. These characteristics are mostly in the head of the therapist. That is, the way a
therapist thinks about a problem and the way that problem
touches him is what determines what strategy will be used to
solve it. For example, an adolescent who refuses to go to school
may be thought of as being disobedient and out of the control
of the parents; or he may be thought of as misunderstood and
mistreated by rejecting parents; or he may be thought of as a
pawn in a struggle between the parents, in which one parent
takes revenge on the other by arranging that the son fail; or he
may be thought of as being concerned about and protective of

the parents, sacrificing himself to keep the mother company and so replacing the father and freeing him for other endeavors; or he might be thought of as the victim of an oppressive school system that is not geared to his sensitivity and talents. All these hypotheses may fit the situation equally well. The hypothesis that is chosen from among the many different ways to think about a problem is the one that appeals most to the therapist at a particular time; it is the one that elicits his sympathy and interest in the family.

The many different ways of thinking about a problem tend to cluster around a set of concepts that are most frequently used in strategic therapy. These concepts are presented here, followed by a review of the various strategies based on these concepts. Each concept tends to encompass a range or continuum that goes from one extreme to another. For example, a therapist might think about relationships in a family in terms of hostility or love, with a range of mixed or ambivalent emotions between the two extremes. But whether a therapist thinks at all in terms of hostility and love instead of, for example, in terms of equality and hierarchy determines what strategy for therapy will be chosen.

In human relations, nothing is ever all black or all white; where there is love there is hate, power is always associated with dependence, behavior is never totally voluntary or involuntary. As soon as one seems to have defined a situation and understood it without ambiguities, the opposite definition comes to mind and appears equally feasible. It may be that what is characteristic of a good therapist's thought processes is a particular tolerance for ambiguity.

The following are eight dimensions for conceptualizing a problem brought to therapy.

Involuntary Versus Voluntary Behavior

Characteristically, the problems presented to therapy are introduced as involuntary behavior by the symptomatic person. The relatives sometimes share this view, or they may prefer to think of the problem as voluntary and under the control of the patient. For example, headaches are often considered involuntary by everyone involved, while stealing cars tends to be considered deliberate, voluntary behavior. Of course, there are exceptions; husbands have been known to argue that their wives deliberately bring on a headache to reject them, and certain parents of delinquents have gone so far as to propose that there must be a specific brain damage associated with stealing mopeds.

A strategic therapist generally prefers to think of all symptoms (except for organic illness) as voluntary and under the control of the patient, although this thought may or may not be shared with the clients. Even with organic illness, often the extent of the handicap is related to this issue of voluntary or involuntary behavior. Sometimes a first step in resolving the presenting problem is to redefine it as voluntary rather than involuntary behavior. This may be the only intervention that is necessary, as the client may solve the problem once he accepts the idea that it is under his control. At other times, the request to deliberately produce involuntary behavior has a paradoxical effect and the behavior disappears. In some situations, a client may present a problem as involving voluntary behavior on his part, and the therapist may choose to redefine it as involuntary and out of the client's control.

The issue of whether a behavior is voluntary or involuntary is crucial to some cases and to some strategies and quite irrelevant to others. For example, defining drug addiction as voluntary rather than involuntary behavior is usually crucial to the therapy. However, whether a couple's bickering is voluntary or involuntary is not necessarily relevant to change.

Helplessness Versus Power

A symptomatic person tends to appear helpless in that he presents unfortunate and/or involuntary behavior that is out of his control; he cannot change even though he wants to. However, this very helplessness is a source of power in relation to significant others whose lives are often limited and dominated by the unreasonable demands, fears, and needs of the sympto-

matic person. The nonsymptomatic members of the family appear to be in a position of power in that their own behavior is
under their control, but they are helpless to influence the symptomatic person, who, in fact, has a great deal of power over
them. Those in power are always dependent on the powerless,
and the helpless have power over the powerful. For example, a
baby can be seen as being more powerful than his mother and
a servant as more dominating than his master.

A therapist can think in different ways about the power
and helplessness of various family members. He may choose to
view the helpless symptomatic child as powerful or as victim-
ized, and the parents may be seen as tyrannical or exploited.
The therapist may or may not choose to share these thoughts
with the family. A therapist thinking within the dimension of
power and helplessness also may choose to redistribute power
and the responsibility that goes with it. Children may become
agents of change, or parents may become therapists to their
children. How a therapist thinks about power and whether he
thinks about power and helplessness at all will determine how
he designs a strategy for change.

Hierarchy Versus Equality

Related to issues of power and helplessness are issues of
hierarchy and equality. Some therapists think that a well-func-
tioning family is an organization of equals, while others prefer
to think that hierarchy is essential to the effectiveness of a family system. Whether a mother and daughter will be organized in
a hierarchy in which one has power over the other or whether
they will be thought of as roommates sharing equal responsibilities has to do with the way in which a therapist chooses to
think about a problem. Deciding whether to shift from hierarchy to equality or vice versa and when to make that shift also
may be at issue in the conceptualization of a problem. For instance, a therapist must decide whether he will consider a marriage to be a relationship of equals or whether he will take into
consideration the hierarchical positions of the spouses in relation to their families of origin and their work situations. A fo-

cus on hierarchy is usually associated with a concern with power, status, money, and extended family. A focus on equality is usually associated with a concern with communication and a view of a couple as an entity separate from extended family and issues in the outside world.

Hostility Versus Love

People can be seen as being motivated mainly by hostility or by love; the same action can be interpreted or motivated by either emotion. A man may reject a woman because he does not like her or because he considers himself unworthy of her and fears that she will not be happy with him. Parents' disciplining of their children can be seen as acts of love or of punitiveness. Some therapists prefer to think in terms of rejection, revenge, punitiveness, aggression, envy, jealousy, hate, and other unsavory motivations. Others go to extreme lengths to see everyone as being concerned about others, benevolently motivated, and compassionate. The issue has to do with both the attribution of meaning and the question of redefinition as a therapeutic tool. Once a therapist understands a problem in a certain way, he has attributed meaning to the motivations of the people involved. This particular meaning constitutes an important consideration with respect to the therapist's choice of strategy. Even more important, however, is whether the therapist's conceptualization of the problem coincides with the view that is presented to him or whether he will choose to redefine and change this view. That is, a rebellious adolescent may present himself as being motivated by hostility and the desire for independence and the parents may see him in the same way. The therapist, however, may think that the young person is benevolently concerned about his parents and distracts them from their other difficulties by providing them with a focus for their concern. The issue then is whether the therapist will choose to explain this view to the family and will base a strategy on this redefinition of the situation or whether he will not explicitly address the issue at all. Strategic therapists tend to think of and redefine people as being benevolently motivated, probably because this view is more conducive to sympathy and interest in the human dramas brought to therapy.

Personal Gain Versus Altruism

A symptomatic person may be motivated by personal gain or by altruism. If the symptomatic person is seen as being hostile, his motivation is always thought to be personal gain. However, if the symptomatic person is seen as being motivated by love, the therapist may view him as being concerned either with helping others or with receiving more affection himself. For example, a symptomatic child may be seen as being concerned about and loving toward parents and siblings. The symptom then may be seen as related to an attempt to receive more affection from them or as an effort to help them by becoming, for example, a communication vehicle between them. The two motivations are not necessarily exclusive. If the therapist accurately perceives whether the child is motivated by personal gain or by altruism, then the strategy of the therapy is laid out before him. All he has to do is to arrange for the same consequences of the symptom to take place without the symptom, and the problem behavior should disappear. For instance, if a child has fears because he wants demonstrations of love from his father, the therapist need only arrange for these demonstrations of love to take place without the fears and the fears will be gone.

Issues of personal gain and altruism are more important in relation to the symptomatic person than to other relatives because a correct understanding of the symptomatic person's wishes can lead quickly to a strategy for change. However, if one considers the possibility that other family members are involved in the problem and are instrumental to maintaining or resolving it, the issue of whether they are motivated by personal gain or by altruism is equally important. If, for example, disability payments for mental illness in one person contribute significantly to the support of other family members, these relatives may be motivated by personal gain to maintain the mental illness of the patient. The therapeutic approach to loving, altruistic parents of a hostile adolescent may be quite different from the approach to parents who seek to arrange a hospitalization so that they can go off on vacation together. However, personal gain and altruism usually overlap and are difficult to distinguish, forcing the therapist simply to choose to think in the way he thinks is more conducive to change.

Metaphorical Versus Literal Sequences

A therapist can focus on concrete facts, observations, and information, or he can be interested in covert, implied, or indirect references. A child who refuses to go to school may be thought of as being a disobedient child and the problem understood as how to get him back in school. In contrast, the refusal to go to school may be considered an allusion to another situation in the family; the therapist may connect it, for example, to the mother's depression and difficulty in finding a job. The child's behavior in relation to the parents may be considered similar to the mother's behavior in relation to the father. The child's refusal to go to school in spite of the parents' efforts may be considered an allusion to and a metaphor for the mother's refusal to go to work in spite of the father's efforts to convince her. The parents' struggle with the child may have replaced the struggle between the mother and father in the family. A therapist may think in terms of the metaphor in a symptom or in a sequence of interaction, yet he still may choose to take a matter-of-fact approach to the therapy, disregarding metaphors. On the other hand, the idea that a symptom may be a metaphor for the problems of another person may lead a therapist to focus on resolving those problems instead of focusing directly on the symptomatic person. If the therapist thinks of the presenting problem as part of a sequence that is metaphorical for another sequence, he may think that a change introduced in one sequence of interaction may have repercussions in other relationships in the family.

Freedom Versus Dependence

A therapist's and client's concern about freedom and dependence may or may not coincide. A therapist may look at a family and think that the members' lives are limited by extreme dependence on each other, or he may find them so unattached that there is minimum contact between family members. Characteristically, certain patients remain intensely attached to their families while the therapist attempts to give them more freedom. Others seem unable to hold on to their attachments and, even though unhappy with their situations, appear to convey that their freedom and independence are more important than any relationships. It is questionable whether it is up to a therapist to say what degree of dependence or freedom is most desirable. Therapists must consider the issue in the context of the goal of the therapy. Sometimes the issue can be considered and discarded. At other times, a redefinition of the problem or the incorporation of the issue into a general strategy is crucial to the success of the therapy. To a person who sees himself as being totally dependent on his family, the therapist may present the idea that he is actually completely alone in the world. A client who thinks of himself as free can be told that he is extremely dependent on his spouse or his children. These redefinitions are possible because freedom and dependence are mostly only illusions. We are dependent on others in extreme and complex ways, yet we are quite alone in the world. The issue of freedom versus dependence has to do with the intensity of human involvements and is usually an important consideration in marital problems and in the difficulties of young adults.

Resistance Versus Commitment to Change

The choice of strategy is often determined by whether client and relatives are seen as resistant or committed to resolving the problem. When family members are not sure whether they like the therapist, whether they will listen to any interpretation of their situation that is different from their own, or whether they want any therapy at all, it is best for the therapist to use indirect or paradoxical methods whose effectiveness is based on the idea that the therapist's influence will be resisted. A restraining technique may be used and the therapist may discuss with the family what the consequences would be if the presenting problem were resolved, implying that these consequences might be negative and that the family is invested in maintaining the symptom (Haley, 1976).

A therapist can expect direct suggestions to be followed only by people who have a certain commitment to change and who are motivated to cooperate with the therapy. When this commitment does not exist, it is usually best for the therapist to plan to bring about change in indirect ways. Most often, people are partially resistant and partially committed to change, and the therapist needs to choose how to view them. Some therapists prefer not to consider the issue of resistance and instead choose to conduct therapy based on the assumption that client and family are committed to change.

Power Versus Weakness in the Therapist

Whether a therapist is in a position of power or weakness in relation to a client and his family determines to a great extent what strategy can be used. A therapist may be in a position of power because of his prestige. Sometimes just working in a well-known institution gives him important leverage. A client or a family may be respectful of a professional and attribute to him wisdom and power simply because he is supposed to be an expert. Other therapists may be too young to be looked upon as powerful. Their professional degrees, their sex, or their ethnic backgrounds may undermine their positions. A client or a family may think of themselves as being more educated or higher in social standing than the therapist. Family and client will usually let the therapist know in direct or indirect ways how much power they are attributing to him.

Generally, direct strategies should be used only when a therapist is in a position of power. It is useless to tell a family what to do if one knows that one's directives will not be followed. Direct strategies include: putting parents in charge of the children by having them enforce rules by following through on consequences if the rules are disobeyed; involving a marginal parent with a disturbed child; assigning tasks designed to improve communication, good feelings, and the organization of the family; prescribing an ordeal (for example, every time a person has an anxiety attack he has to do thirty push-ups); making a contract (for instance, an anorectic will stop taking laxatives if the father stops smoking). These kinds of directives can be given to a family that is motivated to follow them. If the therapist is not in a position of power, he can make a plan to motivate the family to follow his directive before he gives it.

Even when a therapist starts off in a position of power, this power may quickly disappear. An analogy using large organizations may help clarify this issue. A consultant is hired by the owner of a large corporation to improve the efficiency of the organization. The consultant enters the system in a position of power, since he has been hired by the top echelon. Soon, however, he discovers that the problem in the organization is a conflict between the owner and his son, a second-level manager. The son is influenced by his mother, who uses him in her quarrel with her husband over the marketing expert, who allegedly is the husband's mistress. The consultant is faced with a situation in which, to achieve his goals, he must intervene indirectly and diplomatically, as if he had entered the organization from a position of weakness. A therapist's situation is often similar to that of such a business consultant in that he, too, may find himself divested of power when he has to intervene in the upper echelons of a family organization.

When the therapist is in a position of weakness, it is best to use indirect or paradoxical strategies. In playful cooperation with the therapist, family members may be asked to do what appears to be absurd and unrelated to the therapy, and they may become involved in discussions that appear absurd but are therapeutic. A *paradoxical intervention* is a directive or an extended message that is apparently inconsistent with itself or with the purpose of the therapy.* A *directive* is an instruction

---

*This definition is derived from the *Oxford English Dictionary* definition of paradoxical: "Apparently inconsistent with itself, or with reason, though in fact true; also, really inconsistent with reason, and so, absurd or irrational." This definition takes into account the issue of the veracity of "paradoxical." A paradoxical intervention is neither true nor false, but it can be effective or ineffective. If it is ineffective, it becomes "absurd or irrational." Otherwise, it becomes "consistent with reason" because, by solving the problem, it is consistent with the goals of the therapy.

to do something. An *extended message* is a conversation or discussion that may take a few minutes, a whole session, or several sessions.

Most people who come to therapy cannot follow good advice. Most therapists work from a position of weakness with patients who are not particularly eager to follow their suggestions. Usually, clients and families need to be influenced indirectly in order to change. Eight dimensions for thinking about therapy have been described; in what follows, a review of ten paradoxical strategies is presented with case examples and with an explanation of how these strategies relate to the therapist's conceptualization of the problem.* The list is by no means exhaustive and covers only the strategies that have been introduced by the author in this and previous works.

Strategy 1: Asking Parents to Prescribe the Presenting Problem or the Symbolic Representation of the Presenting Problem

In this strategy, the parents of a child with a presenting problem are asked to request that the child purposefully have the presenting problem. Then the parents are to supervise the child in performing the problem behavior and see that he does it correctly. In the case of a firesetter (see Chapter Three), the father was to see that the child set five different kinds of fires a day and that he put them out correctly and safely. The father was a busy man who often worked at night, so sometimes he had to awaken the son in the middle of the night to fulfill this task. The behavior that previously had represented the boy's rebellious destructiveness toward a distant father now came to represent his obedience to an overly involved father. Only after months of setting fires under supervision with no spontaneous firesetting was the task discontinued.

---

*The therapists in the case studies presented in this chapter were Marcha Ortiz, D.N.Sc.; Gerald Hunt, Ph.D.; Patricia Davidge, M.S.W.; Marvin Chelst, Ph.D.; Judy Birch, M.A.; Chip Olhaver, M.S.W.; Rochelle Herman, M.D.; June Kaufman, Ph.D.; Judith Mazza, Ph.D.; Bette Marcus, Ph.D.; Richard Belson, D.S.W.; and Patrick Fleming, M.A.

This kind of paradoxical intervention is similar to paradoxical intention as described by Frankl (1960), to prescribing the symptom as described by Jackson (1963), and to paradoxical techniques presented by M. Erickson (Haley, 1967) and by Haley (1973). However, these authors do not direct the parents to enforce the paradox.* Instead, the therapist gives the paradoxical directive to the child without the participation of the parents. For example, Erickson relates a case of a thumb sucker who was directed to "bug the hell" out of her parents by sucking her thumb. Haley describes the therapy of a boy who masturbated compulsively and who was asked by the therapist to masturbate more frequently on Sunday, the day he enjoyed it most. A schedule was made for masturbating, beginning early in the morning, and the manner of masturbating was determined by the therapist so that the process became an ordeal for the child. Both Erickson and Haley prescribe the paradox directly to the child and do not include the parents in these interventions. In such cases, the response of the parents is unpredictable.

In contrast, when the therapist requests of the parents that they prescribe the paradox to the child, the response of the parents is planned with the therapist, harmful reactions are blocked, the interaction between parents and child around the presenting problem can be controlled by the therapist, and the hierarchy is corrected with the parents, not the therapist, solving the child's problem. The hypothesis behind this kind of paradoxical intervention is that the symptomatic behavior has a certain function in relation to the parents: it is part of an interaction in which the child helplessly persists in his disturbing behavior while the parents helplessly insist that it should end but are unable to stop it. When the parents request the problem behavior instead of trying to prevent it and the child complies, the child is no longer helpless; he is deliberately following the parents' instructions instead of behaving in involuntary ways. The parents also are no longer helpless; they are successful in eliciting the behavior they want from the child. The symptomatic

*Haley (1963) has, however, reported cases where he requested that the husband of an agoraphobic ask the wife not to leave the house.

behavior no longer has a function in the family: it has been replaced by cooperation between parents and child.

After the symptom has been gone for some time, and at
the same time as the paradoxical directive is discontinued, it is
important to move parents and child to a benevolent interaction
around other issues. In the case of the firesetter, for instance,
after a few weeks of setting fires with his father, the boy complained that the two of them should spend time together doing
more interesting and constructive activities. This was denied for
a few weeks, but finally the father was allowed to teach his son
how to play a musical instrument and to study history with
him. In this case, the paradoxical directive was given to the father to enforce, and the mother was the log keeper who reported to the therapist. This was appropriate because the father
was distant from the son, who was an only child and craved his
father's attention. In other cases, it might be appropriate to
have the paradox enforced by the parent who is more involved
with the child or by both parents simultaneously.

In a similar approach, the parents are requested to ask the
child to perform behavior that is a symbolic representation of
the presenting problem. Symbolic representation refers to behavior that is similar to the symptom by vague suggestion rather
than by exact resemblance and that could be taken by an observer to represent the symptom. Then the parents are to supervise the child performing correctly the symbolic representation
of the problem behavior. If the actual symptomatic behavior oc-
curs, more symbolic representation is prescribed.

A twelve-year-old girl masturbated compulsively at home
as well as at school, in front of the whole classroom. The behavior consisted of sitting on the edge of her chair and rubbing her
genitals against the corner of the chair with a movement that
was very noticeable and that could be felt by the children sitting in adjacent chairs. The mother first noticed that the child
was touching herself when she was five years old. Alarmed, the
mother took her daughter to her gynecologist, who performed a
pelvic examination, apparently for the purpose of determining
whether there was an infection. The traumatic effect of this
examination on the child is not known. By age nine she was

masturbating in the classroom. The teachers were concerned but sympathetic, and the child was in individual therapy for three years. When she entered seventh grade and a new school, her classmates became upset with her behavior. Their parents complained, the school psychologist intervened but was unable to produce any change, and the girl was expelled from the school. At the time she was referred by the school psychologist to family therapy, she was studying at home with a tutor. The girl's family consisted of the mother, who was a nurse, the father, who was an office manager, and an eleven-year-old brother.

In the first family session, the child was asked to perform the symptom as she did in school. Chairs were set up as make-believe school desks, the brother acted as a classmate, and the therapist played the role of teacher. The girl refused to perform in front of the parents; they had to turn around so she could demonstrate for the therapist. Then the therapist talked with the girl about her interests. She wanted to work with handicapped children when she grew up, and the therapist emphasized how nice it was to meet a young lady like her who wanted to be a helper. The therapist asked each parent to tell the girl that it was all right for her to masturbate in private, that it was only wrong to masturbate in public. The girl answered that she knew that. It was established that the goal for the therapy was that the child stop masturbating in public; however, the parents would not object to her masturbating in private. Then the therapist told the parents that she would embark on the treatment of this problem only if the parents promised in advance that they would follow all her instructions and continue to come to therapy for at least ten weeks, even if their daughter objected. The parents promised to do so, and the therapist explained that this problem was complex both in its origins and in its consequences for the girl and for the family. However, it was clear that the girl had not gone through the proper developmental stages, since she was behaving in ways that were more appropriate to a five-year-old than a twelve-year-old. Therefore, the parents had to take her back to an earlier stage until she was mature enough to move on to other things.

With this introduction, the following instructions were

given. The parents were immediately to buy a rocking horse of the old-fashioned kind that was made of some sturdy material. Three times each day—before going to school, when she came home from school, and in the evening—the girl was to sit on the rocking horse and rock for half an hour. The parents would take turns supervising her rocking and would make sure that she was not reading, watching television, or doing anything else but rocking. In this way, the girl would be practicing behavior that was appropriate to an earlier stage of development and would not need to practice those behaviors at school. The therapist would contact the school and arrange for the immediate reinstatement of the child, and the parents would send her to school from then on. The parents would enroll the girl in ballet, gymnastics, and horseback riding with teachers that were serious and exacting so that she would be involved in interesting activities every day after school and learn new ways of disciplining her body. If the school reported that the girl had masturbated, the time on the rocking horse would be increased to three one-hour sessions for that day; in addition, the girl would have to run around the yard for fifteen minutes on a broomstick rocking horse, supervised by her father. The parents agreed to all this, and the girl was amused by the idea of the rocking horse and delighted with the lessons she would be getting. She was a pixieish little blonde who had been excruciatingly shy during the interview and had only answered the most simple questions after looking at her mother for permission. The only time she had not been shy was when she had demonstrated the masturbation.

By the next interview one week later, the parents had carried out all the directives. For the next two or three weeks, the girl only masturbated in school for a few minutes the day before coming to the therapy interview. The therapist told the father to call the school and inform them that from now on he was in charge of his daughter and that he would call them every week for a report on whether she had masturbated. Also, a new consequence for masturbating in public was set up. For each time that she masturbated, the girl had to spend four hours of the weekend writing an essay under the supervision of one or both parents. Also, if she squirmed in her chair while writing the essay in ways that were reminiscent of masturbation, she had to write another essay for another four hours. However, if the school reported that she had behaved well during the whole week, the father would take her and a girlfriend to a movie while the mother went out with the brother. (The child had been withdrawn and marginal during all her school years, and it was important to encourage social relations through these outings and with the private lessons, through which she could make new friends.)

After this, the girl masturbated in school only once, and the weekend consequence was enforced. She enjoyed rocking on her horse and did it without complaints. The therapist discussed with the family how, as the child became more normal, she might begin to misbehave in ways that normal girls misbehave; for example, she might begin to tease her younger brother. This could cause a problem, since she was now strong from so much ballet and gymnastics. It was suggested that the boy should take up some sport that he might enjoy and that would prepare him to defend himself against his sister. He chose karate and was very pleased with it. This intervention shifted some attention to the boy and prevented him from feeling neglected.

As the girl became more normal and no longer masturbated publicly at home or at school, the mother began to complain about her misbehavior. The child had shifted from being very shy, obedient, and extremely dependent on her mother to being impudent, disobedient, and belligerent. The parents asked to see the therapist alone and the mother, in tears, explained this situation. The therapist sympathized with the mother and said that the father should take charge of his daughter as he had done in relation to school. The mother would refrain from punishing her or arguing with her but would keep a chart on which she would draw an unhappy face every time the girl misbehaved. When the father came home in the evening, the mother would report to him. If there was one unhappy face on the chart, the father would supervise the girl in some household chore as a consequence of her misbehavior. If there were two or more unhappy faces, the father would punish himself instead of punishing his daughter. This punishment would consist either of doing some unpleasant household chore that the mother usually did, such as cleaning the bathrooms or the kitchen, or of taking the mother out to dinner to an expensive restaurant and leaving the children to prepare dinner for themselves. And, as the therapist explained to the father, since the girl loved him dearly, this would be the worst punishment for her: to see her father performing an unpleasant chore or spending money recklessly in a restaurant. From the father's sacrifice, the girl would learn self-discipline. The father agreed to follow the instructions, the mother was pleased, and the children were called into the room and informed of the plan. During the three years that the girl had masturbated in public, the mother had suffered the most pain and humiliation, because it was she who always dealt with the school. If the symptom served some function of hurting the mother or if the father were setting the child up to hurt the mother, then this function would be blocked by making the father the one to contact the school and later by making him be the one to suffer the consequences if the girl misbehaved—particularly if these consequences involved helping the mother with her chores or taking her out to dinner.

After this, the girl's misbehavior disappeared and she became very cooperative. Her appearance also improved and she looked more grown-up and feminine. In a final session, the children planned that the parents should do more together and go dancing, which the mother liked, and bowling, which the father preferred.

When prescribing the presenting problem itself is questionable because it may encourage the symptom rather than have a paradoxical effect, or when practical or ethical concerns are involved, prescribing the symbolic representation of the presenting problem is indicated. Once the symbolic representation of the symptom is accepted, the paradox works in the same way as directly prescribing the symptom: The response of the parents is planned, harmful reactions are blocked, parent-child interactions are controlled by the therapist, and the hierarchy is corrected by the parents as they solve the problem. Parents and child first become involved in a struggle over the symbolic representation of the symptom, then the function of the real symptom disappears, as well as the real symptomatic behavior, and eventually the struggle over the symbolic representation gives way to other interests.

This type of paradoxical intervention is indicated particularly in cases in which the presenting problem is involuntary behavior—that is, in cases in which numerous attempts to change the child's behavior have been made and in which the child has said that he would like to stop but cannot. The intervention does away with both the involuntary nature of the behavior and the parents' helplessness to change it, both of which are essential ingredients in maintaining the symptom.

Another situation that calls for this kind of intervention is one in which the only benefit from the symptom seems to be an expression of hostility by the child and negative consequences for the parents. These interventions address the issue of the antagonism between parents and child. The function of the symptom is changed so that, instead of causing negative consequences for others, the symptom or its symbolic representation becomes an ordeal for the child herself.

This intervention bears some resemblance to an approach described by Erickson (Haley, 1973). He tells of the case of a boy who compulsively picked at a sore on his forehead. The father, angry because the boy persisted in this behavior, had broken the child's most treasured possessions, a bow and arrow. Erickson recommended that the boy practice penmanship for several hours a day. Because the child would be so busy with his writing, the father had to do all the son's chores. Erickson describes this approach as prescribing the character trait rather than the symptom. The boy compulsively picked at his sore; now he would compulsively write instead. The directive had negative consequences for the father and provided a way for the child to get back at him. In contrast to performing the symbolic representation of the symptom, practicing penmanship and picking at a sore are similar in that they can be considered compulsive behaviors, but one does not represent or appear to be similar to the other.

Strategy 2: Prescribing the Pretending of the Symptom

In this paradoxical intervention, the therapist asks the parents of a child with a presenting problem to request that the child pretend to have the presenting problem. The parents are to criticize the performance and make sure that the pretending is accurate, and then they are to behave as they usually do when the child presents the real problem behavior.

A young woman from a wealthy family had been a patient in mental hospitals for the ten years since her parents' separation and divorce. In the many hospitals in which she had resided, she had accumulated a variety of diagnoses, including epilepsy. She had arrived at the University Hospital in an ambulance, accompanied by her father, and she was being given antiepileptic medication intravenously because her seizures were so frequent and uncontrollable. It was arranged that the parents would come together on a weekly basis for family therapy sessions. A variety of strategies were used to solve this young woman's problems, but prescribing the pretending of the symptom solved the problem of the seizures. The parents were told to ask her to pretend to have a seizure in the session and then to reassure and comfort her. The staff of the ward where she was hospitalized were instructed to do the same. At first the young woman complied, but soon she refused to collaborate and was exasperated at the idea of pretending to have seizures. So, at any sign of irritability or impoliteness from her, parents and staff were instructed to say: "Oh, good! You are pretending to have a seizure!" and proceed to reassure and comfort her. The seizures disappeared within two weeks and recurred only once or twice a year during the next three years. The hypothesis behind the intervention in this case was that the seizures served the function of bringing the girl closer to her father, of bringing the divorced parents together in therapy, and of giving her special privileges in the hospital, since demands could not be made of her because she was so sensitive and any upset could bring on a seizure. If the girl could get special attention from the pretend seizures, then the real seizures would no longer be necessary. In such cases, it is important for the therapist to be prepared to deal with other attempts the young person might make to remain in a privileged position after the presenting problem disappears. As new problems are presented, similar or different techniques can be used.

This kind of paradoxical intervention is appropriate when the presenting problem is involuntary behavior and when the therapist understands the interpersonal gain and the dependence on others derived from the symptomatic behavior. If this bene-fit is understood, then the therapist need only arrange for the same benefit to be accrued without the occurrence of the pre-senting problem. Pretending to have the symptom rather than actually having it accomplishes that objective. This approach is indicated when the interpersonal gain is benevolent and consists of receiving demonstrations of affection, togetherness, or spe-cial privileges that are not harmful to anyone. However, this intervention should not be used if the benefit involves hurting someone or expressing hostility. Arranging for such benefits to occur even if the symptom disappears could hardly be consid-ered helpful. When the therapist understands the benefits from the symptom in terms of hostility, Strategy 1 should be used; when the benefit is understood in terms of an attempt by the symptomatic person to gain love and special consideration, Strategy 2 can be used.

Strategy 3: Prescribing the Pretending of the Function of the Symptom

In this approach, the family members perform, in a play-ful way, actions that represent what the therapist believes to be the function of the symptom. These actions do not literally rep-resent the function of the symptom but are a condensed, abbre-viated, somewhat symbolic, and somewhat humorous version of the family drama. A special characteristic of this type of para-dox is that it reverses the positions of family members with re-spect to who needs help and who is helpful. For example, if a daughter is suicidal, the mother is asked to pretend to be de-pressed and the daughter to help the mother; if a child has fears, a parent may be asked to pretend to be afraid and the child to protect the parent. The therapist conceptualizes the function of the symptom in terms of a parent covertly asking for help and a child covertly helping the parent through symptomatic behavior. In the playful prescription of the paradox, the parent overtly asks for help, and the child overtly helps the parent.

In the case of a boy with nightmares and night terrors, the mother had recently remarried; her new husband was an older man who was very reluctant to become involved with her children—to the point of actually saying in a session that he was not and did not want to be their father. He was kind to them and they found him appealing because he was an interesting man, but he insisted on keeping them at a certain distance. The biological father lived far away. The mother was struggling to develop a career and had a tendency to be obsessive in her doubts about the well being of her children and about the decisions she had made in her life. She described herself as an anxious and fearful person. The fears of the child were approached by asking the mother in the session to pretend that she was very afraid because she had seen a cockroach (the mother had previously expressed her fear of bugs). The stepfather was then to call the boy: "Jimmy, to the rescue!" Together, hand in hand, they would run to the mother and the boy would stomp on the cockroach. Then they would play another scene in which, instead of being afraid of a cockroach, the mother was afraid of a thief (played by a sister) who was breaking into the house. Once more the stepfather would call: "Jimmy, to the rescue! We must save your mother!" Together, they would repel the intruder. The family was asked to repeat these performances several times in the session and to act them out every evening at home. The idea behind the directive was that the child's fears were a metaphor for the mother's fears and that the mother was covertly asking the child to help her in integrating the stepfather into the family and in eliciting from the stepfather the kind of concern that she wanted. The child was covertly helping the mother by developing a symptom that brought the whole family to a therapy where these issues were discussed. In the dramatization that was prescribed, not only was the mother overtly requesting the child's help and the child overtly helping her, but the child was doing so in collaboration with the stepfather, holding his hand and participating in an action that the stepfather initiated. This togetherness between the stepfather and son was what the mother wanted. Her fears centered around the distance between her son and her husband. In the next session, the stepfather told the therapist that he understood the intervention and that the dramatization was no longer necessary. He and the boy would find more interesting things to do together. The symptom did not recur.

Another example is the case of the suicidal sisters (see Chapter One), in which the father, by appearing extremely depressed, was covertly requesting his daughters' help in preventing his wife from leaving him and the girls, by attempting suicide so that the mother could not leave, were covertly helping the father—or so it was that the supervisor understood the function of the symptom. A playful dramatization made evident the father's depression and the daughters' concern and enabled the father to spontaneously correct his relationship both with his daughters and with his wife.

This kind of paradoxical intervention is appropriate when the presenting problem is either involuntary or voluntary behavior and when the therapist understands that the gain the child derives from the symptom is being helpful to someone else (usually one or both parents), even though this helpfulness is unfortunate. If the therapist understands not only the child's gain but also the covert request made by others for the child's help, then the strategy is simply to elicit an overt, rather than covert, request from those others and to have the child help overtly rather than through symptomatic behavior. Pretending to help the parents in other absurd ways (through dramatizations both in and outside of the sessions) rather than in the absurd way in which the symptomatic behavior is helpful serves this purpose and matches in playful ways the creativity of the symptom. This intervention is indicated when the therapist can see that the child is motivated mainly by love and concern, but it should not be used when all the therapist can see is rebelliousness and hostility (not because the intervention could cause harm, but because the family will refuse to collaborate). In

Strategy 2, the benefit for the child is understood as an attempt to gain love for himself; in this approach, the benefit is an attempt to gain a positive effect (reassurance, togetherness, love) for someone else.

The success of this kind of intervention depends in large measure on how accurately the therapist's understanding of the function of the symptom matches the child's reality. If the match is not good, chances are that the child will be reluctant to collaborate. For example, in the case of the suicidal sisters (Chapter One), when the supervisor at first misunderstood the situation as one in which the girls were helping the mother, the girls were very reluctant to perform the dramatization. However, as soon as the father was asked to pretend to be depressed and the girls to pretend to help him, they jumped out of their chairs, eager to perform the scene. A clear understanding of hierarchy and of metaphorical sequences is also crucial to this approach.

In another case, a little girl was afraid of taking shots (which she needed for her school immunizations). The family was from the Middle East and had suffered during a war in which the children had witnessed bombings and shooting. Ideas about the double meaning of the word "shot" were explored, and the parents' situation in a new country was discussed. It was found that the mother was Iranian and Jewish and so felt doubly persecuted. The father did not speak English and was facing the problem of having to revalidate his professional degree before he could begin to aspire to the same status he had enjoyed in his native country.

In spite of the father's difficult situation, the supervisor thought that the daughter's fears were a metaphor for the mother's fears and an attempt to help her by getting the father to be more involved with and more caring toward the family. So the mother was asked to pretend to be afraid of shots while the daughter pretended to give her a shot (a toy nurse's kit was brought into the session for this purpose) and the father consoled the mother. The daughter, however, refused to participate in this scene, persisting in her refusal even when the scene was performed several times anyway, with her sister playing the one who gave the shots. The mother collaborated but did not like her part, and at the end of the session she told the therapist that it would be simpler to go ahead and force the child to take the shots that she needed for school, since it was too much for a mother to have to go through this kind of ordeal. The therapist responded only that he would like the family to perform this scene every evening at home for a week. (This child had been referred by the child psychiatrist at a clinic where a pediatrician and nurses had failed to give her the necessary shots because of the child's tantrums and screaming.) That week, after the one therapy interview, the parents took the little girl to the clinic and told her she must have her shots, which she took quietly and rather cheerfully—but, during the process, the father fainted. While he was recovering and the clinic staff was making sure that he had not had a heart attack, a nurse taught the girl how to give injections, and the girl even practiced on some oranges. The father's reaction at the clinic was an indication that the problem had been misunderstood and that the child's fears were most likely metaphorical of the father's situation and an attempt to help *him* and not the mother. Because of this misunderstanding, the child had refused to collaborate in the pretending and the mother had been reluctant to participate.

An intervention that is similar to prescribing the pretending of the function of the presenting problem is prescribing the symbolic representation of the solution to the presenting problem. This was the approach described in Chapter One in the case of the diabetic mother and daughter. In that case, the mother was neglectful of the child and did not give her the care she needed as a diabetic. The mother was asked in the session to pretend to be a nurse and, dressed as such, she went through all the motions of giving her child the care her medical condition required. She was instructed to do the same at home and, in representing a nurse, she was able to care for her daughter in ways in which she had failed as a mother.

The daughter had been covertly helping the mother by putting her in contact with physicians in the hospital. The daughter was asked to take care of her mother's diabetes while pretending to be a nurse and in this way to express her concern overtly. In their dramatizations, both mother and daughter were symbolically representing the solution to the problem by taking care of each other in appropriate ways. Instead of expressing her love for her daughter by refusing to demand anything unpleasant of her (and thus neglecting to care for her diabetes), the mother, representing a nurse, took care of her child. The daughter, as a nurse, also took care of her mother instead of expressing her love by getting herself hospitalized.

This intervention is an indirect approach to therapy in that the mother was not asked directly to take care of her daughter; she was only asked indirectly to take care of her in a make-believe way. The daughter, by pretending to be a nurse, was asked to do in an overt way what she had been doing covertly by getting herself hospitalized—to take care of her mother. The mother responded to the situation by taking charge of her daughter and of herself, which was exactly what the therapist was after. This solution also points out another paradoxical aspect having to do with a hierarchical reversal: When the child was asked to be a nurse to the mother, the mother responded to this reversal of the hierarchy by correcting it and behaving responsibly.

This kind of intervention is indicated when family members fail to perform simple behaviors or to assume responsibility that could easily be assumed. It is appropriate when the benefit of the presenting problem appears to be related not to hostility but to love and concern. The intervention allows a solution to the presenting problem to develop and provides a way for this love and concern to be expressed.

Strategy 4: Prescribing a Reversal in the Family Hierarchy

This paradoxical intervention consists of putting the children in charge of the parents. All the children (or one particular child) are asked to take charge either of the parents' lives in general or of one aspect of their lives, such as their happiness (see Chapter Three). Sometimes the therapist gives the children authority by putting them in charge of each other, in this way replacing the parents. The children might be asked to discuss what they would direct a parent to do if they were in charge of the parent's happiness (see Chapter Three). This approach is appropriate when the parents present themselves as incompetent, helpless, and unable to take charge of their children while complaining that the children are out of control. It is also appropriate when a parent presents disturbing behavior, such as delinquency, alcoholism, or drug addiction, that disqualifies him from a parenting position. As the children are put in charge (in practice or in fantasy), the parent responds by becoming more caring and effective. The intervention is paradoxical because the parent typically complains that the children are "out of control," meaning out of the control of the parent, and the therapist responds by putting the children *in* control of the parent rather than *under* the control of the parent. The therapist prescribes a reversal of the hierarchy, which leads the parents to take charge and correct the hierarchy by taking more responsibility for themselves and for their children.

This approach is useful when a parent is ineffective, although it is not necessary to understand why the parent is ineffective. It is necessary, however, to give the family some rationale for putting the children in charge. The rationale might be, for example, that the parents are unhappy and need to be taught how to be happy or that a parent is tired and needs to be relieved of responsibilities. Whatever the rationale, the children need to be given concrete tasks and concrete topics to discuss in the sessions in relation to the parents. Most of the content of the therapy interviews must be centered on the children taking charge and on how they are going to do this. The approach is particularly useful when the parent does not provide appropriate caring behavior, when child abuse or neglect has occurred, or when the parent is the presenting problem. It is particularly indicated when the children are seen as being concerned about and caring for the parent but rejected in their affection. Whether the children are asked to take charge in realistic or fantasized ways, the tone of the sessions should be light, benevolent, and humorous.

As the children give love to the parents (by actually giving them directives, by taking care of them, or by fantasizing about how they would take care of them if they could), the parents not only become more responsible and caring toward the children but they also resolve their own problems. Children are often surprisingly wise in their directives and advice and, with the therapist's encouragement, they can be very helpful. When the children are put in a position of authority, it is important to allow them to make positive suggestions and to forbid all criticism of the parents. In this way, cross-generational coalitions that divide the parents and support their disturbing behavior are blocked, and a child cannot express overtly a parent's covert criticism of the other parent. At the same time, an alliance between the children is encouraged so that they can support each other and need not seek coalitions with the parents. This, in turn, gives the parents the satisfaction of seeing that their children are strong, united, and benevolently concerned about each other and about the parents, all factors that contribute to the improvement of the parents' situation. As the parents improve, the children are happy to see that their efforts have succeeded and they have helped their parents. With increased self-esteem and competence, the children, who characteristically have serious problems of their own, often spontaneously resolve their own problems.

This approach is appropriate both with shy, withdrawn children and with rebellious, misbehaving ones. It can be used with young children, adolescents, or young adults. No matter how withdrawn the child or how disruptive his behavior, the approach can succeed if the therapist is able to appeal to the child's sense of humor or to touch the chord of love that can always be found between parents and children. The strategy is especially useful when parents are very rejecting, because little or nothing is expected from them and all demonstrations of love and concern are initiated by the children.

The approach of prescribing that the children take charge of the parents is paradoxical when used in situations in which the parents are covertly encouraging the children to be in charge because of the parents' incompetence, symptomatic behavior, or neglect, or because one parent is siding with the children against the other parent. The therapist encourages the children to take charge in an effective, benevolent way—quite differently from the way in which the parents were covertly requesting that the children take charge. As the therapist's prescription makes this covert request by the parents overt, the parents react against the therapist's prescription and take charge of themselves and of their children. The therapist appeals to the love between parents and children, to the children's altruism, and to their ability to communicate in metaphor.

Strategy 5: Paradoxical Contracts

This strategy consists of tying together two problem behaviors in two different family members so that if one person engages in symptomatic behavior the other is encouraged to do the same. The hypothesis is that the person with the presenting problem is trying to help another family member through the symptomatic behavior. If the situation is reversed so that the symptomatic behavior is harmful rather than helpful to the other person, and if it is nonsymptomatic behavior that actually helps the other person, the symptom will disappear.

A family consulted because their nineteen-year-old daughter was starving herself. During the previous year, she had eaten less and less, exercised violently, and abused laxatives; at present, she had locked herself in her room, too weak to move. She had refused to see a physician or a therapist, and the parents, in desperation, decided to consult a family therapist. The young woman refused to come with them, but they brought an older daughter, who had married and moved out of the home. They wanted to know how they could get treatment for their anorectic daughter.

Before the first interview each family member was seen individually in what was then a standard procedure at the Family Therapy Institute. Each was asked what was the problem about which they were consulting, and they all said it was Martha, the anorectic daughter. When asked if there was another problem about which they were concerned, the mother and sister said that they were extremely concerned about the father.

He had had bypass heart surgery, and he was an alcoholic who would not stop drinking. He drank large quantities of hard liquor every day, even though he knew that it would kill him, and he refused to admit that he was an alcoholic. In fact, the mother and the daughter, Susan, insisted that the subject not even be brought up in the session because the father became extremely hostile.

The therapist went into the first session prepared to engage the family to the point at which the father's alcoholism could be discussed openly without fear or hostility. After finding out the details of Martha's problem and learning something about the family's way of life, the therapist asked the parents and Susan the following question: If Martha were worried about someone in the family, about whom would she be worried? It was important to find out, said the therapist, because sometimes young girls express their concern in strange ways, and Martha might be acting so strangely because of her preoccupation about someone she loved. The father then said that he had had bypass surgery and that Martha might be worried about his drinking. A discussion followed about the father's stress at work, his illness, and his drinking. At the end of the session, the therapist obtained the parents' permission to visit Martha at home that afternoon shortly after the parents went back to their house. The therapist said that she was concerned that Martha's situation could be life threatening and that she wanted to see her and do her best to help her.

When the therapist arrived at the house, the father was coming in through the door with a big brown bag full of liquor bottles. Martha was locked up in her room. The therapist knocked on the door, and Martha refused to open it. The therapist explained through the door that she was concerned about the young woman's health and would like to speak with her. Martha answered with a barrage of insults and abuse. The therapist went back to the living room and told the father that she thought she knew what to do to get Martha to start eating again but that she needed the father's cooperation. The father agreed to cooperate. The therapist then said that she would like to make a contract between Martha and the father. If the father

drank even one glass of alcohol a day, Martha could starve herself; if the father did not drink a drop of alcohol, Martha had to
eat. The father accepted this agreement, and the therapist went
back and told Martha (through the closed door) that she had a
deal that she thought would interest her. Then she proceeded to
explain the contract and the fact that the father had agreed to
it. Martha said, "Just a minute. I'm going to get dressed and
come out." She came out, shockingly emaciated, and said to the
therapist, "I still think you're a bitch, but I'll go along with the
contract."

     The father stopped drinking, and Martha started eating.
The therapy took several months, during which the parents,
with the support of the therapist, struggled to get Martha back
to a normal way of life, involved in work and with friends. She
never came to the therapy, but the father gave up the drinking
and the daughter's weight returned to normal.

     Contracts between family members can be used in a vari-
ety of ways, some straightforward and some paradoxical. To
say that if the daughter eats then the father does not drink
would be a straightforward contract; the daughter would be re-
warded for eating in a direct way by helping her father stop
drinking. This is quite different from saying that if the father
drinks then the daughter can starve herself. Here the burden of
the responsibility is placed on the father. If he drinks, he is sacrificing his daughter. If he does not drink, he is saving her life.
If the father stops drinking but the daughter continues to starve
herself, she is sacrificing her father, since she knows that drinking will cause his death. The contract is set up so that the drinking of the father has the power to destroy the daughter and the
anorexia of the daughter has the power to destroy the father.

     Straightforward contracts, in which good behavior is re-
warded and interpersonal benefits are obtained, are frequently
used in family therapy. Paradoxical contracts are more unusual.
Another example of a paradoxical contract is the case of a
young, single mother and her thirteen-year-old son. The mother
brought the child to therapy because he was doing poorly in
school, getting bad grades, and the school psychologist had recommended psychotherapy. The boy explained to the therapist
that he had intellectual inhibitions and a learning disability, as

had been demonstrated by the psychological tests that he had taken at school. He had an anxiety that prevented him from doing his homework. The boy was very verbal and obviously intelligent. He seemed to take pride in his knowledge of his psychological difficulties. The mother was very young and attractive and led a lonely life. She worked all day and spent the evenings at home with her son, who kept house and cooked for her. She had had a boyfriend, of whom the child had been fond, but had broken up with him a year earlier. The therapist asked the mother what expectations she had for her son, and she explained that she wanted him to be a good student and to be successful. He asked the boy what kind of life he would want for his mother, and the boy said that he would like to see her happier, seeing friends and going out more. Then the therapist asked the mother if she would be willing to accept a contract that he would set up between her and her son that would ensure the child's success in school, even though it would require some sacrifice from the mother.

She said that she would do her best to help her son. The therapist said that she had to accept the contract before knowing what it was, and she agreed. The therapist explained the contract: Every time the boy brought home a B or an A on his homework, a test, a quiz, or whatever, the mother had to go out that evening with a man. It did not matter who the man was, where she went, or how long she stayed out, but she had to go out for a certain period with a male friend. If she failed to do so one day, then she had to do it the next day. The son would stay home and take care of the house. The mother said that she did not know whom she could call to go out, and the therapist told her that she should start thinking about it right away because the son might bring home a B any minute. The boy appeared to like the contract right away. It was written, signed, and witnessed by the therapist. The boy immediately began to bring home A's and B's, and his inhibitions and disabilities disappeared. The mother was too embarrassed to call a strange man and invite him on a date, so she decided that it would be less painful to call her old boyfriend, since at least she knew him. As a result, they got back together again.

This level of paradoxical intervention is appropriate when

the presenting problem is either voluntary or involuntary behavior and when the only gain the symptomatic person seems to derive from the symptom is being helpful to someone else by bringing him to therapy. The alcoholic father of the anorectic girl and the lonely mother of the boy with the school problem came to therapy because of the problem of the child. Apart from that, there was no evidence that the symptomatic behavior was helpful to anyone in any way. Before using this intervention, the therapist must ask himself the following questions: Is the symptomatic person trying to help someone else who has a problem? Does the symptomatic behavior help because it puts this other person in contact with a therapist? Does the therapist understand the problem of this someone else that the symptomatic person is trying to help? Is this someone else kindly motivated toward the symptomatic person and willing to make an effort to help him or her? If all the answers are affirmative, then the contract can be set up.

This type of intervention is best used where there are strong emotional ties and a serious commitment to one another. The success of the intervention largely depends on how accurately the therapist understands the emotional bond between the participants. The approach should not be used if all the therapist can see are hostility and unsavory motivations.

Special contracts between therapist and family members can also be of a devious nature. A working-class family consulted because of a suicide attempt by one of their ten-year-old twin boys. The father, a steel worker, who at the time was mostly laid off from work, customarily beat his children. He had threatened to whip the boy with a belt, and the child had taken a bottle of the mother's Valium. The boys were firesetters, misbehaved in school, and had been through years of therapy for their alleged hyperactivity. The father was uncooperative and said that he did not want to come to the sessions. The mother said that if her husband did not come, she would not come either, since previous therapy with only the children and her had failed. Both parents were very negative with respect to the children. They talked, for example, about the twins' stealing, but when questioned, what they considered stealing was taking cake from the refrigerator. An important goal of the therapy was to control the father's violence toward the children; related to this was the issue of helping the parents discriminate between abnormal behavior and normal misbehavior of ten-year-old boys. A first step in curtailing the father's violence toward the children was to help him have a more positive view of them instead of indiscriminately interpreting their behavior as bad, delinquent, crazy, or out of control. Toward this end, several indirect techniques were used. At the end of the first interview, when the therapist was discussing the fee, which was on a sliding scale, the father said that he could not pay and that they could not come to the therapy. The therapist said that she would make a deal with him. If he followed her instructions (she had given him several directives for things to do with the children), but reported the following week that the children had misbehaved in abnormal ways, then *she* would pay for the session out of her own pocket. If the children had not misbehaved in abnormal ways, then the father would pay the lowest fee on the sliding scale according to the family's income. The therapy was taking place at a university hospital, where the therapist was a psychiatric resident. She said to the father that it was important for him to keep this contract secret because if anyone knew that she was paying for the sessions she would get into very serious trouble; in fact, she would have to give him the money every time so he could pretend that he was paying with his own money and no one would be aware of their arrangement. The father, who was a proud man, said that he could not accept such an arrangement and would not have her pay for the therapy. The therapist said that it was very important to her to be successful with his boys and that she was betting on the idea that she would never have to pay because their behavior would improve so quickly. The father accepted, and the parents never again talked of the boys' taking food, bickering with each other, and so on, as abnormal misbehavior. They followed the therapist's directives, and the firesetting and disturbed behavior disappeared. The therapy continued for seven months and shifted to a focus on marital problems. The therapist only had to pay for two sessions.

Strategy 6: Prescribing Who Will Have
the Presenting Problem

This paradoxical intervention consists of prescribing the symptom but changing who will have it. Another family member is asked to take over the symptom for a time or various family members are asked to take turns in presenting the problem. The therapist makes the request with the rationale that if other family members were to take over the problem behavior (delinquency, hostility, depression, and so forth) the family member with the presenting problem would be free to engage in other pursuits. The idea is that not only is it fair to take turns but in this way old family habits will not be disturbed, since other family members will continue to be preoccupied with someone —but that person will be different from the identified patient. It is best for the therapist not to specify concretely which problem behaviors someone else must take over but to present them in a broad generalization, such as referring to being "the life ruiner" (see Chapter Two). In this way, the therapist equalizes different kinds of disturbing behavior and does not find himself in the questionable ethical position of prescribing antisocial acts. The therapist does not expect the family members to actually follow the paradoxical prescription; he expects them instead to rebel against the absurdity of such an assignment. This kind of paradox is similar to the first uses of paradox in the 1960s in that the family is expected to resist the therapist, but it is different in that this resistance is not thought to be related to the therapeutic effect. Rather, it is the interaction with the therapist and between family members that evolves from this prescription that brings out the conflicts in the family so that they can be resolved. Because the therapeutic effect lies in these discussions, it is important when using this approach that the whole focus of the sessions be centered on the issue of taking turns and who will have the problem, as illustrated in Chapter One with the case of The Life Ruiner. The therapist should be prepared with long monologues and discussion of why it is important to take turns, how it is helpful to various family members, who should have the problem, and so on. The fact that family members refuse to follow the paradoxical instruction should lead to more discussion of whether they did or did not follow it, the importance of doing so, and so forth.

This kind of paradoxical intervention is appropriate in cases of severe problems, such as antisocial behavior, drug use, delinquency, bizarre communication, and depression. The hypothesis is that the person with the presenting problem is a metaphor for someone else in the family, distracting from the conflict with that person in a way that is unfortunately benevolent in that it prevents the resolution of that original conflict. As family members discuss the instruction to take turns, there is the implication that they replace each other and are interchangeable and that they collaborate with each other in causing distress. This disagreeable idea leads the individual members to assert their separate identities and insist on positive rather than negative collaboration. The therapist then takes the position that, although this would be desirable, it has not been their usual way. The conversation eventually leads to an eruption of the conflict for which the presenting problem was a metaphor and which it replaced. At this point, the therapist should focus the session on this conflict and attempt to resolve it so that it no longer will be dealt with in metaphorical ways.

Another important aspect of this type of intervention is that, as the family members agree to discuss the possibility of taking turns in having the problem, they also accept the idea that the symptomatic behavior is voluntary and therefore can be changed. Once this is accepted, the interaction around the problem is never the same, and improvement follows naturally.

Taking turns is a technique that seems easiest to use in a relationship between peers, such as siblings or spouses, but it also can be used across generations. Haley (1982) tells of a therapy, inspired by the case of The Life Ruiner, in which the father of a severely depressed young woman was asked to take over her depression for a week so that she could be free to pursue other interests. The father willingly sat in his daughter's chair and proceeded to become extremely depressed. It was then found that he had serious problems and that his depression was not make-believe. The daughter had been helpful to him in that her depression had made him pull himself together in order to help her and had brought him to therapy. The depressed father, eager to help his daughter, offered no resistance to the idea of taking turns.

This level of paradoxical intervention is appropriate when the problem is severe and presented as either voluntary or involuntary and when the therapist understands that the gain for the symptomatic person consists of helping someone else or detracting from another conflict, even though who is being helped or what conflict is avoided may not be clear. This is a very verbal therapy, and the therapist must be prepared to talk at length in benevolent but absurd ways, matching with wit the creativity of the symptom. The approach should not be used if all the therapist can see are hostility and unsavory motivations. In Strategy 3, the benefit for the symptomatic person is understood as an attempt to gain a positive effect for someone else. Here the benefit is understood as an attempt to detract from conflicts with other family members or from the problem of another family member. The success of the intervention does not depend on an accurate understanding of the function of the symptom, but it does depend on a general understanding that the symptomatic person is a metaphor and that the symptomatic behavior is metaphorical for other conflicts. The approach results in transferring the family conflict back to its origin. In so doing, hierarchical problems are resolved and power is no longer derived from helplessness.

Strategy 7: Prescribing the Presenting Problem with a Small Modification of the Context

This paradoxical intervention consists of prescribing the presenting problem but changing when, where, and how it will occur. In this way, the therapist introduces a change that appears to be minor but that in fact alters so much the context in which the presenting problem takes place that it disappears. The approach originated in the work of Milton Erickson (Haley, 1967, 1973; Zeig, 1980). If the therapist wishes to give a rationale for this directive, he can say that it is an interesting experiment or that the presenting problem is so important that it is necessary to assign for it a special place, time, and rules for its manifestation. Family members are expected to follow the paradoxical prescription and to report their experience to the therapist. The therapeutic effect is related to the different interaction that evolves between family members as they follow the therapist's instructions. Since interactions with others are part of the context of symptomatic behavior and since the context makes possible the existence of the presenting problem, then changing the context can render the symptomatic behavior impracticable.

This kind of paradoxical intervention is particularly appropriate for marital problems in which husband and wife are stuck in a repetitive pattern of unfortunate interaction that does not seem to hold any benefit for either spouse. If the couple respond with humor at the absurdity of the directive (see Chapter Two), the therapist should respond with a deadpan attitude and only covertly imply that the directive is in fact humorous, so as not to disqualify it.

The hypothesis is that the nonsymptomatic spouse collaborates in the presenting problem and "sets up" the other spouse. Changing the when, where, and how of the problem behavior makes it impossible for it to occur as a response to some message of the other spouse; a specific time, place, and manner are prearranged so that one spouse can no longer set up the other. Changing the how of the presenting problem changes the response of the nonsymptomatic spouse so that he or she can no longer contribute to the persistence of the problem. The therapist's instructions about how the problem should take place should lead to blocking communication and discouraging interaction. As the couple carry out the instructions over a period of weeks, they strive for increased communication and positive interaction, which is exactly what the therapist is after.

In this approach, the benefit of the presenting problem for the symptomatic person is understood as being a leftover from the past, when the symptomatic behavior probably had a metaphorical function and sustained the other spouse or detracted from other conflicts. In the present, the problem is understood as part of a habit-forming, repetitive sequence. The success of the intervention does not depend on an accurate understanding of the previous function of the symptom, but it does depend on a general understanding of the interaction around a presenting problem as a part of the problem. Issues of metaphorical communication, hierarchy versus equality, and hostility versus love are relevant to this approach.

A therapist can use this approach when he can understand the roots of the presenting problem but not its present function. As the interaction between the spouses changes, there is usually an eruption of the current conflict for which the presenting problem is a metaphor. For example: A couple in their sixties came to therapy because the wife could no longer tolerate her husband's constant recriminations and harassment for an affair she had had thirty years before. The husband said that he needed to express his pain for what she had done to him. The wife said that his expressions of pain were verbal abuse that on occasion had even become physical abuse. The therapist suggested that it was important for the husband to express his pain and for the wife to listen to him with sympathy. A special time, place, and manner in which this would happen would be set up. Every evening, the couple would sit together in the living room and the husband would express his pain for the terrible thing that the wife had done to him. The wife would listen sympathetically but would only answer, "I'm sorry, dear." This interaction would take place at 5:45 P.M., before the Walter Cronkite newscast, and would end when Walter Cronkite appeared on television. It would also occur in the morning from 7:45 to 8:00 A.M., before breakfast. In this way, the husband would be able to express his pain and the wife to give him her sympathy without interfering with breakfast or dinner or their favorite television program. While apparently favoring increased communication and the expression of old resentments, the directive was in fact blocking communication (since the wife could only say, "I'm sorry, dear") and reducing the expression of the husband's resentments to an absurd fifteen minutes before Walter Cronkite. The couple followed the directive successfully for two weeks, and then a conflict erupted.

The wife, instead of answering "I'm sorry, dear," bitterly recriminated the husband for a platonic affair that he allegedly was having. It became apparent that the wife was intensely jealous and that the couple's interaction around the wife's affair of thirty years ago was a metaphor for their conflict around the husband's relationships with other women. The therapy proceeded to another stage, in which rules were negotiated about relations outside the marriage and the husband wrote and signed a solemn promise to abstain from any relationships of which his wife was not a part.

Strategy 8: Paradoxical Ordeals

This intervention consists of making a deal between family members so that certain behaviors have unexpected consequences. The consequences of the symptom become that which the symptom was developed to avoid. An example is the directive given to the couple in the case of the compulsive cleaner (see Chapter Four). After getting the couple to agree that a cleaning woman, such as the wife, should have normal work hours, from nine to five o'clock, they were given the following instructions: If the wife was involved at all in cleaning after five in the afternoon, except for doing the dishes after dinner for half an hour, the husband would force her to lie in bed with him and watch television for the rest of the evening. If the cleaning occurred before dinner, he would take her out to a nice restaurant that evening. If the woman cleaned during the night, the consequence of either lying in bed or going out to dinner would be applied the next day. The hypothesis on which this strategy was based was that the woman cleaned to avoid being with her husband. By arranging that if she cleaned she had to be intimately involved with her husband, the consequences of the symptom became exactly what, through the symptom, she was trying to avoid.

The approach has its origin in Milton Erickson's case (mentioned earlier in this chapter) of the boy who picked at a sore on his forehead (Haley, 1973). In that case, the father, exasperated because the boy would not stop doing this, had broken the child's favorite possessions, a bow and arrow, but the boy's behavior had not improved, and he had continued to pick at his sore. Erickson gave the child the task of practicing penmanship with the same obsessiveness and compulsion with which he picked at his sore. Also, since the child would be so busy practicing his handwriting, he told the father that he would have to replace the boy in doing all his chores. Erickson describes this case in terms of replacing one obsessive-compulsive trait—picking at the sore—with another—practicing handwriting. However, there is also the implication that if the child was engaging in this self-destructive behavior in order to punish his father, he could still do so by practicing handwriting, since the father would have to do the chores; but this new behavior would have no negative consequences for the child himself.

The case of the compulsive cleaner and the case of the boy who picked at his sore are similar in that both have to do with obsessive-compulsive behaviors. They differ, however, in that in Erickson's case one compulsive behavior is replaced with a more constructive one that has negative consequences for another person and in the case of the compulsive cleaner the compulsion is not replaced with another obsessive behavior. Instead, based on a hypothesis about the function of the symptom, it is arranged that the consequences of the obsessive behavior be what the obsessive behavior was designed to avoid—proximity to the husband.

An ordeal is not necessarily paradoxical. Arranging that the consequence of a symptom be the performance of a task or act that is more painful, difficult, or unpleasant than the symptom itself is a nonparadoxical ordeal. An example would be directing a patient who suffers anxiety attacks in the middle of the night to get up from bed and spend an hour writing a difficult report that then must be presented to a supervisor. An ordeal is paradoxical when, as in the case of the compulsive cleaner, a consequence for the occurrence of the symptom is arranged that is implied to be a punishment for the patient but that is actually harmless and benevolent and brings family members closer together. The elements of harmlessness and benevolence, however, are not sufficient for the success of the ordeal. The directive must be based on a correct hypothesis of the interaction the symptomatic person is trying to avoid (although he cannot admit to this avoidance). Going out to dinner or getting into bed with the husband can hardly be considered a fitting punishment for a compulsion as annoying as compulsive cleaning. Giving the directive, however, implies a punishment while never explicitly stating it as such. If the directive is enforced, the benevolent interaction that is aversive to the patient can only be avoided by not engaging in the symptomatic behavior. But the ordeal itself can hardly be thought of as aversive, and in this lies the paradox.

This kind of paradoxical intervention is particularly appropriate for marital problems in which one of the spouses presents fears, anxiety, or compulsive behavior. The benefit for the symptomatic person is understood as an avoidance of the spouse, and the success of the intervention depends on an accurate understanding of the function of the symptom. This intervention is not only useful when the symptomatic person is trying to avoid someone but also when the presenting problem is related to an attempt to get back at someone, to make someone suffer or pay, or to take advantage of others. The symptomatic person is sometimes a resentful burden rather than a benevolent helper of the family. In such cases, the therapist can set up an ordeal that appears to be designed as a deterrent for the symptomatic person but that in fact is designed to cause trouble and difficulties for the other family members. In this way, the therapist can indirectly arrange that other family members endure suffering because of the therapeutic directive and thus make it unnecessary for the symptomatic person to cause this suffering through the symptom.

A thirty-year-old woman had been a compulsive vomiter for fifteen years (she also had had periods of alcoholism and drug addiction). She had lost all her teeth from the acid brought up by the vomiting, and her health was not good. She did not work but was supported by her father, a physician, who gave her large sums of money to the detriment of his other seven children. The young woman, who said she vomited because of conflicts with her parents, played on her parents' guilt and took advantage of them. Many interventions were used over the course of therapy, which lasted three years. A strategy that was particularly successful was the prescription of a paradoxical ordeal. The mother was instructed to keep in her house large amounts of the junk food the daughter liked to binge on (cheap ice cream, Oreo cookies, fried chicken, and so on). Every day, the young woman was to come to the mother's house, and the mother was to put all the junk food on the kitchen counter and supervise the daughter as she mushed up all the food with her hands. When the mother was satisfied that the food was properly mixed together and looked as if it had been digested, the daughter was to take the food to the guest bathroom and flush it down the toilet. While this task was being performed, one of the other family members always would be present, even if it meant having to leave work to do so. If the mother on occasion could not carry out the task, one of the siblings would replace her. If the toilet clogged after throwing the food in it, a plumber could not be called; the father had to unclog the toilet. The therapist gave this directive to the family with the rationale that what the daughter had been doing was throwing away food that had gone through her stomach first. Why not throw it away directly, which would be much less costly to her health? The family members were told that they had to participate because the daughter loved them and needed their help. In this way, under the guise of caring and togetherness, the family members were given an ordeal that replaced the pain that the vomiting had caused them. The incidence of vomiting decreased remarkably and eventually disappeared through the use of this and other similar interventions.

Paradoxical ordeals can be used, as described above, to maintain the interpersonal benefit derived from the symptom while making the symptom unnecessary. They also can be used to eliminate the interpersonal benefit so that the symptomatic behavior no longer achieves the same purpose. One way to arrange this is to reverse the sequence in which the symptomatic behavior takes place. For example, the husband of a compulsive vomiter (who binged secretly and then vomited) was told that every time his wife vomited he was to tenderly take her by the

hand to the kitchen and then, while always affectionately holding her hand, he was to force her to stuff herself. If she vomited again, the sequence had to be repeated (Madanes, 1981b).
In this way, the sequence was reversed—instead of vomiting
being the consequence of bingeing, bingeing became the consequence of vomiting—and the whole sequence came under the
supervision of the husband.

Paradoxical ordeals work best in cases of compulsive behaviors and when client and family are clearly committed to
resolving the problem. "We want to solve this problem but we
cannot do it" is the kind of statement the therapist needs to
hear before prescribing a paradoxical ordeal.

Strategy 9: The Illusion of No Alternatives

Generally, therapists like to broaden their clients' horizons, developing complexity so that the same sequences of behavior do not have to be rigidly repeated and introducing alternatives into otherwise limited lives. Paradoxically, however,
broadening the horizons of some clients can best be accomplished by limiting their choices and presenting an illusion of no
alternatives. Some people are talented, beautiful, intelligent,
and well liked, and the apparently unlimited possibilities that
loom in their future actually limit their possibilities by making
them constantly unhappy with what they have in the present.
It is not possible to have everything at the same time. For such
a person, for example, choosing a spouse makes it immediately
apparent that another possible spouse could have been chosen
from among the myriad of men or women potentially available.
If one career is followed, there is always the possibility that another career might have brought even more success. Sometimes
such a person is paralyzed and does nothing but think about
whether he made the right choice in the past and only broods
about what choice to make in the future, without actually making one. This perspective is best broadened by limiting choices
and presenting an illusion of no alternatives.

An ambitious young husband had a demanding job, and
his beautiful, intelligent wife constantly nagged him for not

spending more time with her. She had had a successful career but had quit working when she married and at the time of therapy was only taking some crafts classes. The husband was a busy politician who could hardly cut down his work time. The wife was not happy with her situation, but she could not make up her mind about whether she wanted to lead a leisurely life, have children, devote herself to crafts, return to pursuing her old career, or start a new career. Therapist and supervisor decided to follow the strategy of the illusion of no alternatives. The couple was told that the wife had the problem of not being able to make up her mind about what career to follow—whether to be a professional woman and put all her energy into a career in her field or to have a career as a wife and devote all her energy and creativity to her husband. Both careers had their appeal and their advantages, but, because she could not decide between them, she did not follow either one and she was a failure in both. In terms of her professional career, she was doing nothing; and, although she pretended to be following a career as a wife, she was in fact ambivalent and undecided and was consequently also doing nothing in that respect. Other women who followed a career as a wife helped their husbands with their work. Why did she not go to her husband's office and volunteer to work? With her intelligence and experience she could be very helpful. Wouldn't the husband agree? The husband said yes, he would agree. Why did she not give dinner parties for important people to further her husband's career? All she needed was to learn to make three or four good dishes that she could then repeat. If she were serious about a career as a wife she would be doing that, and surely she could do it as intensely and successfully as other women. She was very attractive, and she was charming. She could use that charm in flirting with her husband's important business contacts so that they would be more interested in him and would help him. The therapist added that, of course, it could be that she was not seriously pursuing a career as a wife because she was thinking that it would be best for her to go back to her professional career; that might be best, the therapist said, although perhaps she thought that as a professional woman she would not be able to have children and to be a good mother. That very well could be, although the therapist herself had three children and had raised them successfully while holding a job as a researcher. But the therapist really thought that the wife was more inclined toward a career as a wife because of her devotion to her husband. Because she was afraid of making that decision, and because she hesitated and was torn, she did not do anything well. However, the therapist thought that it was very important for the wife not to rush into any decision and to spend some time thinking and consulting with her husband about the problem of her career choice: a professional career or a career as a wife.

Two weeks later, the wife said that she had decided that she did not want to have a career as a wife; she wanted to have a professional career. The therapist restrained her, saying that she should not rush into a decision that might be too hurried. The therapist said she suspected that this was not her true choice because if it were she would have done something about it in all the time since she had quit work. Within two weeks of that session, the wife had a very good job and was working full blast. The couple were much happier together, but they wanted to consult the therapist about how they could reconcile the wife's work commitments with the husband's so that they could spend time together without sacrificing their work. The therapist said that they had resolved other problems in the past and so they could resolve this one. They were at least as intelligent as the therapist and did not need her help. The wife called a few months later to tell the therapist how happy she was and to thank her for "changing her life."

The two mutually exclusive alternative careers presented by the therapist were purposefully limited and not quite truthful. There are all kinds of life-styles, and many different combinations are possible in terms of being a wife, a mother, and a career woman. However, an illusion of no alternatives was presented to make it easier for the wife to make a choice. While she was in fact living as a not-very-devoted full-time wife, the implication that she could choose to be a devoted wife as a career provoked her into deciding what she wanted to be. As she became more involved in her profession, she stopped wondering about her choice of husband and about how she could change him. She also became less demanding of him. As the wife became more involved in her work, the husband began to want to spend more time with her, and they achieved a better balance in which they were both equally interested in each other.

The illusion of no alternatives is an approach that is useful in dealing with life's difficulties, not necessarily with symptomatic behavior. It is useful in getting people unstuck from an illusion of freedom that makes choice impossible. Issues of personal gain versus altruism and freedom versus dependence are relevant to the approach.

Strategy 10: The Illusion of Being Alone in the World

Usually therapists like to be optimistic and hopeful and to bring people together with good feelings and expectations of increasing cooperation and love for each other. Sometimes, however, to encourage expectations of love, caring, and support not only may be unrealistic but may limit the options in a client's life, restrict opportunities, and increase bad feelings. Some severely disturbed people seem to have dedicated their lives to devious helpfulness toward their loved ones. For this sacrifice, they expect in later years to be unconditionally cared for and supported. However, those who elicit such devotion and self-destructive helpfulness tend not to retribute in kind, so the patients find themselves let down and rejected by those from whom they expected the most. Recriminations then lead to more rejection, which in turn leads to extreme behavior and further rejection. Usually, it is a disturbed child and his parents who are involved in such a chronic drama of resentment and rejection, although sometimes spouses can be caught in the same kind of interaction. A benevolent family therapist may unwittingly help the parties further entrench themselves in their respective positions. As the therapist requires responsible dedication from the parents and they refuse to provide it, their rejection becomes more apparent. The more the parents refuse to comply with the therapist's requests, the more the disturbed young person behaves in helpless and dependent ways. This helplessness, however, only elicits more rejection on the part of the parents. The therapist is caught in a cycle in which the more he pushes the parents to behave responsibly and in caring ways toward their offspring, the more the youth behaves helplessly and incompetently and the more the parents become rejecting. The issue for therapy is how to break this escalating cycle of bad feeling, incompetence, and failure. One way is to present to the family the idea that the youth is alone in the world, that the parents have rejected and abandoned him, and that, for all practical purposes, he is an orphan.

A sixteen-year-old boy had been arrested for stealing a car. He was an alcoholic and had dropped out of school. His drinking was supported financially mainly by his grandmother, for whom he did odd jobs and who denied that he had any problems. His mother was a sad, obese woman, and his father, who appeared to be very much a ladies' man, was too busy to be involved with the family. During several family sessions, small, simple things were requested of the parents, particularly of the father, in an attempt to arrange that he provide some guidance for his son and some help in finding him a job and getting him into night school. The parents never complied with any requests or directives. The grandmother attended one session, during which she refused to collaborate with the family or the therapy in any way.

It was apparent that the boy provided some distraction to the mother while the father was out gallivanting around. He was not about to give up the boy as a means of keeping his wife off his back. Father and son came alone to the sixth session, and the father once more reported that he had not done anything for his son. The therapist said that, unfortunately, he was going to have to tell the boy the truth about the way he saw his situation. Looking at the boy and ignoring the father, the therapist proceeded to explain that he was shocked at the father's total lack of concern for his son, that the young man had to realize that he was alone in the world and that he could not count on his father for anything, including emotional support, financial support, and guidance. He, the therapist, had done everything possible to elicit some interest or concern on the part of the father and had totally failed. In terms of the mother and grandmother, the youth had nothing to count on either; they were not interested in helping him. If the young man were to end his days in the gutter or make something of his life, it would depend entirely on him; nobody was going to help him, he was alone in the world, and it was up to him. The therapist was sad that this was the situation, but he felt he owed it to the young man to tell him the truth about what he saw. The therapist ended the session by saying that he would continue to see the boy alone if he wished but that he was no longer interested in the family. Through all this, the father did not say a word. The boy enrolled in night school, quit drinking, and found a job. The therapist continued to see him alone every two or three weeks for a few months. He brought his girlfriend, a very sweet, attractive girl, to the last session.

Another example of this approach is the therapy of a twenty-six-year-old woman from a well-to-do family who had been a patient in mental hospitals since she was sixteen years old. Among many other symptoms, she was severely suicidal and on several occasions had cut her wrists and hurt herself. The parents were divorced and involved in a struggle over money, with the father feeling that the mother was always extorting money from him. The mother was depressed and alcoholic. After a year of family therapy, during which various approaches were used for different problems, the young woman was out of the hospital and living with her mother. She could not find a job, however, they had little money, and the father kept making promises of the help that he would give his daughter, but this help never materialized. The therapist called a session with the mother, father, and daughter. Before this session, supervisor and therapist wrote a letter, which was addressed to the father and was intended for him to read aloud when he came to the interview. In the letter, the therapist said that the father had constantly disappointed both the therapist and the daughter by always promising that he would act as a responsible, caring father to the daughter and then refusing to do so. These promises that were not kept were very detrimental to the young woman's well being. The father sometimes talked as if she were his daughter, but then he refused to give her the things that a woman her age, in her social class, and with her family situation should have. The father did not give her money, would not buy her clothes, or offer her help or guidance. The therapist had decided that it was necessary once and for all to clarify the situation. The father had to decide either that he would be father to his daughter and give her the things that went with that relationship or that he would not be her father, which meant deciding that she was an orphan. If he decided not to be her father, from then on he would disappear from her life and she would go on by herself, as an orphan.

Father, mother, and daughter were shocked and could not quite believe that that was what the letter actually said. The father said that he certainly would be father to his daughter and that he was not dead. He would help her find a job and an apartment, pay for her education, buy her clothes, and do everything that was necessary. Mother and daughter were pleased, and a plan was made specifying how all this would take place. A month later, nothing had been accomplished and the father had managed to fail to provide anything. Another meeting was held and the father was confronted with the fact that, although he had chosen to be a father to his daughter rather than be dead in relation to her, he had failed to fulfill any of his promises. The father made excuses about the girl's misbehavior and attempts to obtain money for her mother through him. He ended by saying that he would not help her and she should consider him dead. The therapist said that now that he was dead and she was an orphan, she had to inherit from him. He needed to know what the estate consisted of, because he would get in touch with the other adult children to make it clear that the young woman was taking her part of the inheritance. The father immediately backed off and said that that was being too literal; he had not really meant that he was dead for his daughter, and she could count on him and he would help her. From then on, without the therapist's intervention, he provided some help and financial support, and, in contrast to the past when he had been inaccessible and most often refused to speak to her, he became always available to her on the telephone and in person when she wanted to see him. Most important of all, the daughter changed and began to expect very little or nothing from him. She stopped hoping that her father would be more generous to her mother and began to see him more realistically for what he was. She found a job and a boyfriend, with whom she moved in. Two years later, she still had some hope that she could get some money out of her father, but she was independent and working and had not gone back to the mental hospital.

Just as freedom is an illusion, it is also an illusion to think that we are alone in the world. At some level, even the most rejecting of parents care for their children, and there is always someone one can turn to for help. However, to achieve the goals of therapy, it is sometimes better to insist that the client is on his own, alone in the world, and that he must rise or fall on his own merit rather than insist on improving relationships in futile attempts to make people act responsibly toward one another.

This approach should be used only in chronic cases in which all other approaches have failed and in which there is an ongoing intense relationship between therapist and family. The therapist needs to think about the problem in terms of helplessness and power, hostility and love, and freedom and dependence. A therapist should be wary of using this intervention simply out of sympathy for the offspring and irritation with the parents. It is an intervention that could be harmful and should be used only by the most experienced therapists.

Conclusion

When a therapist sees himself as being in a position of power, he can directly tell a client or a family what to do to solve the problem. When a therapist is not certain that his directives will be followed, he is better off using an indirect approach to influence people. This chapter presented eight dimensions or variables to consider in attempting to understand a dilemma brought to therapy and described ten paradoxical strategies, with indications for matching the therapist's mode of thinking to each particular strategy. The emphasis, however, is on the therapist's thoughts rather than on the strategies. When a therapist thinks clearly about a problem, he can develop the right strategy to solve it.

References

Allen, S. *Funny People*. New York: Stein and Day, 1981.

Erickson, M. "Indirect Hypnotic Therapy of an Enuretic Couple." *Journal of Clinical and Experimental Hypnosis*, 1954, *2*, 171-174.

Frankl, V. "Paradoxical Intention: A Logotherapeutic Technique." *American Journal of Psychotherapy*, 1960, *14*, 520-535.

Haley, J. *Strategies of Psychotherapy*. New York: Grune & Stratton, 1963.

Haley, J. (Ed.). *Advanced Techniques of Hypnosis and Therapy: Selected Papers of Milton Erickson*. New York: Grune & Stratton, 1967.

Haley, J. *Uncommon Therapy*. New York: Norton, 1973.

Haley, J. *Problem-Solving Therapy: New Strategies for Effective Family Therapy*. San Francisco: Jossey-Bass, 1976.

Haley, J. Personal communication, 1982; 1983.

Jackson, D. D. "A Suggestion for the Technical Handling of Paranoid Patients." *Psychiatry*, 1963, *26*, 306-307.

Landau-Stanton, J., and others. "The Extended Family in Transition: Clinical Implications." In F. Kaslow (Ed.), *The International Book of Family Therapy*. New York: Brunner/Mazel, 1982.

Lederer, S., and Jackson, D. D. *The Mirages of Marriage*. New York: Norton, 1968.

Madanes, C. "Protection, Paradox and Pretending." *Family Process*, 1980, *19*, 73-85.

Madanes, C. "Family Therapy in the Treatment of Psychosomatic Illness in Childhood and Adolescence." In L. Wolberg and M. Aronson (Eds.), *Group and Family Therapy 1981*. New York: Brunner/Mazel, 1981a.

Madanes, C. *Strategic Family Therapy*. San Francisco: Jossey-Bass, 1981b.

Marquard R. *Jokes and Anecdotes for All Occasions*. New York: Galahad Books, 1977.

Minuchin, S., Rosman, B., and Baker, L. *Psychosomatic Families*. Cambridge, Mass.: Harvard University Press, 1978.

Montalvo, B. *A Family with a Little Fire*. Videotape training film, Philadelphia Child Guidance Clinic, 1973.

Penn, P. "Multigenerational Issues in Strategic Therapy of Sexual Problems." *Journal of Strategic and Systemic Therapies*, 1982, *1*, 1-13.

Selvini Palazzoli, M., Cecchin, G., Prata, G., and Boscolo, L. *Paradox and Counterparadox*. New York: Aronson, 1978.

Selvini Palazzoli, M., and others. "Hypothesizing-Circularity-Neutrality: Three Guidelines for the Conduct of the Session." *Family Process*, 1980, *19*, 3-12.

Zeig, J. "Symptom Prescription and Ericksonian Principles of Hypnosis and Psychotherapy." *American Journal of Clinical Hypnosis*, 1980, *23* (1), 16-33.

Index